Blue Butterfly

Blue Butterfly

WALKING THROUGH GRIEF ON THE PCT

Linda Bakkar

ISBN: 1543153607
ISBN 13: 9781543153606
Library of Congress Control Number: 2017902500
CreateSpace Independent Publishing Platform
North Charleston, South Carolina

Dedicated to the memory of Adnan M. Bakkar
1936 – 2014

Linda and Adnan Bakkar sharing a scarf at a Seattle Sounders soccer game.

Contents

Introduction

SNUG IN MY SLEEPING BAG, I opened my eyes to dim light filtering through the tent fabric. I was not alone on the ridge. Several other thru-hikers had camped between the bushes, but mine was the only tent. I liked to start my hiking day in the early morning, when the coolness of the air kept energy levels from sagging. Stretching, I rose to pack my gear.

The thru-hikers who camped under the stars had less to gather, and I called out to them as they took to the trail and left me by myself among the trees.

Outside I extracted the tent stakes from the ground, one by one, counting them as I circled around the corners of my shelter. One was missing. I searched the area with my headlamp, thinking I had passed it by, but I could not find it.

The previous night, the force of the wind had made it difficult to find a protected spot for camping, and I had tried a couple nearby locations without success. Maybe I had dropped one of the stakes during the attempts. I wandered around with my head down, searching the ground, and rammed my head into the pointed end of a broken branch.

Ouch! That hurt! I thought.

Turning my focus back to the search, as if it had not happened a minute ago, I jabbed my head on the same broken branch again, this time so hard that I had to sit down on a bent-over tree trunk to wait for the pain to subside. Words flew into my mind like a gust of wind.

You must accept *the loss.*

I had lost the tent stake, but the words scraped my newly wounded soul with fresh waves of pain.

You must accept *the loss.*

I did not take it to mean the loss of the tent stake but the loss of my sweet husband, Adnan, who had died a few weeks before from pancreatic cancer. I dissolved in tears, keening my grief. That is what I was here for…to walk through the beginning stages of grief surrounded by the beautiful, wild landscape of the Pacific Crest Trail.

Throughout the next couple of months, the trail would give me comfort as well as teach me lessons to help me face the future alone. This is my story… the story of how the trail helped me navigate my way through the wilderness of being a new widow.

Half of My Heart

CHAPTER 1

The Wrenching

I HELD HIS HAND IN both of mine and watched his fingertips turning blue. His erratic heartbeat and gasping breaths still held his fragile, decimated body in the hospital bed in our back bedroom, but his pain was gone. Our physician son, Asem, had shown me the clinical signs, and there was no reaction to any type of pain stimulus. It could be hours, or it could be minutes, but pancreatic cancer was wrenching half of my heart out of me, taking the love of my life away, after forty-eight years of a good, solid marriage. Surrounded by loved ones, my husband was finally getting free of his failing body. His chest heaved one last time, and his heart stopped beating. Asem looked at his watch to note the time of death, having been able to detach himself from the fact that this was his father, who had taught him how to be a man. It was almost midnight. I kissed my sweetheart one last time and left the room, heading straight for the back door, to seek a small trail in our woods behind the toolshed. Under tall cedar trees, I screamed my rage at the universe for taking my love from me. I yelled at my beloved, asking him why he had to leave me. Tears and snot flew in every direction as I walked in the dark, raving with fury and disbelief. After some time the emotions drained, and I stuffed the empty spot in my heart with the cotton of numbness, returning to the house where my bewildered family waited. They understood my reaching for the outdoors for comfort, yet they seemed relieved when I returned safely to the bright lights of the kitchen. Memories of our life together formed a flickering tapestry of bright times mixed with dark. Their father had been such a force, a Presence, in any room. It was inconceivable that he could actually be gone.

I was still a teenager when I met him in college at the University of Wyoming. After knowing each other for just two weeks, we had fallen hopelessly in love and decided to get married. We had our wedding during semester break, three months later. Adnan was my husband's name. Even after forty-eight years, I could never really pronounce it right. My American accent could not get the guttural sound of it correct.

Over the years we had our share of disagreements, but through constant communication, we talked them out and grew closer together. He finished college in the School of Engineering, and several years later we were a family of five. Adnan made a good living as a design engineer for the Boeing Company. He worked there for thirty years, sacrificing his desire to live in his own country, Syria, for the comfort of his wife and sons, and he took American citizenship early in our marriage. Our three sons grew up in this house full of memories.

Adnan was a devout Muslim. He served on the board of trustees for the Idris Mosque in the Northgate area of Seattle, Washington, where we lived. Every Friday he attended services there, but I did not go with him. My own faith was deep, but I did not like to go to the mosque. I preferred to go out into the beauty of a mountain meadow or stand at the base of a crashing waterfall to worship.

Adnan's other passion was scouting. All our boys became Eagle Scouts, with Adnan at the center of their scouting lives. Even after the boys left home to the Marine Corps, to college, and to families of their own, Adnan stayed involved with scouting, helping countless young men to the rank of Eagle. During his illness, scouting friends came to the house to help me with some of the outdoor chores and to say good-bye, leaving the house in tears. Adnan had been aware of their visits, but now the moment of his passing had come.

Asem, our firstborn son, was in his last year of a five-year surgical residency in the city of Phoenix, Arizona. The medical program directors gave him leave to fly to Seattle to come to our home in Lynnwood, just north of the city, to be with his dad. With him he brought his daughter Asemah, our eight-year-old granddaughter. His ex-wife, Katy, had come, too, for a few days, but she could not stay long. Asem had kept my husband pain-free for the last two weeks, with just enough medicine to relieve the discomfort, but not enough to take away my husband's mind and awareness. Now Asem took over the duties of notifying the mortuary, the mosque, and the hospice organization that had supported my husband through his last weeks of illness.

Responding to Asem's call, members from the mosque drove from Seattle in the middle of the night to do what they could for all of us, and I was especially appreciative of their presence, as the trauma to my soul was so profound that I was unable to function or even answer questions. I felt paralyzed, as if the whole situation was unreal. Asem, perhaps because of his training, knew what to do after a death from disease, but it could not have been easy for him either. The part of my heart that was his mother reached out to him with silent prayer.

Tameem, our second son, lived just a few miles from our house, and he had been able to spend more time with his dad than his brothers could. On the night of Adnan's death, Tameem came over to help, while his wife, Reid, stayed home with their two little girls, five-year-old Saphira and nine-month-old Kiara.

Rasheed, our youngest son, was a commissioned officer, a helicopter pilot for the US Marine Corps, based at Camp Pendleton, just north of San Diego. The marines allowed him to come home for three weeks to be with his dad. His wife, Lydia, along with five-year-old Ina and three-year-old Desmond, came up as well to be able to say good-bye. During those weeks Rasheed had close talks with his dad and was able to convey his deep love. "Where is Rasheed?" was my husband's question to me several of his last mornings while he could still talk. On this night, Lydia and the kids were at Tameem's house with Reid and the girls. Now, in the kitchen, Rasheed turned his focus toward his brothers, toward me, toward my husband's brother Azzam, and toward Tammy.

Tammy had been like a daughter since Tameem had introduced her to us years before, back when they had coached a high-school swim team together. She lived in South Lake Tahoe, in central California, and was able to arrange her work schedule to come up to our home for almost seven weeks, during which time she took over the household. She loved her *Baba* (Arabic for "father"), and she loved me, too. She cooked, did the dishes and laundry and even cleaned the bathrooms so that I could spend time at my sweet husband's bedside holding his hand. Because of Tammy, Adnan and I could stare into each other's eyes for hours at a time. *Oh, his beautiful chocolate eyes!* The house, crammed with people in every spare room, was not neglected. We all had what we needed, thanks to Tammy. Her parents, who lived nearby, were frequent visitors as well and provided love and support for all my family.

Azzam, Adnan's brother, had flown to our city from his home in Cincinnati. He was a retired airline pilot and a naturalized American citizen like my husband. Adnan was comforted by his brother's presence and by Azzam's quiet reading of the Koran by the bedside. Azzam also used his phone to help Adnan communicate with relatives on the other side of the world using Skype. Even when my husband could no longer talk, he could still hear his sister's voice from Syria.

Mohammad (we called him "Hamudi") lived near us as well. His father, Nader, was Adnan's and Azzam's oldest brother, but Nader lived in Saudi Arabia and could not be with us. Hamudi brought his wife, Inaz, to the house during my husband's illness, her musical voice reading from the Koran bringing peace into the room, and we felt their support and love deeply.

Muslim friends came and went, like the scouters. One evening, the sheikh came to visit. He was the imam from the mosque, whose leadership and religious knowledge were well respected by the people who attended it. I could see Adnan visibly relax after the sheikh had come to see him and pray for him by the bedside. Like the scouters, the Muslims left the house in tears. None of us wanted this. None of us wanted to have to say good-bye to this wonderful man, the man who was my heart. Yet now…he was gone.

As we stood in the kitchen together, close family and close friends, all of us in shock that such a time could actually happen, Asem helped the hospice nurse to prepare Adnan's body for the mortuary, and I felt like I was in a dream world. His death had been noted at 11:30 p.m., on March 10, 2014. Islam dictated that he must be buried before sunset on March 11. Asem took the necessary steps to get the process going so that his dad could be properly buried in Islamic tradition. It was very late by the time Adnan's body left our home for the last time, wheeled out the front door in a body bag on a stretcher, and we each tried to catch a few hours of sleep.

The fog and numbness were still with me in the morning. The empty spot in my very center gnawed away at my heart, and disbelief swirled around my brain. I should be able to go downstairs to greet my husband's smiling eyes and have our morning hug, a daily ritual we had observed throughout our marriage...

Nothing.

The emptiness was heavy in the house. But showers and the activity of getting ready for the burial had begun, and I mechanically ate the breakfast Tammy had put out for us on the dining-room table. All the colors and flavors of life were dull this morning. Things needed to be done, and I did them by rote.

Asem and Azzam left with one of the Muslims to accompany my husband's body from the mortuary to the mosque and then to the cemetery in the Snohomish Valley, fifteen miles to the north. Rasheed donned his best formal military uniform, a Marine Corps tradition, and waited with me for the call from Asem to let us know when to leave for the cemetery. (Adnan had chosen a cemetery in Snohomish for his grave. A few weeks earlier, I asked him why he hadn't chosen the one that was within walking distance of our house. He told me it was too expensive—always, to the end, thrifty with our finances.)

Reid's cousin Ashley stayed with the young children at their home while the adults of my family (including Asemah, who Asem deemed old enough to understand the proceedings) participated in the Muslim burial, and after the call, we all left the empty house to head for Snohomish.

The Woodlawn Cemetery sits on a hill that overlooks the green valley of the Snohomish River. Our car was one of the first to arrive, well before the hearse. A circular road winds through the expanse of green grass, and soon cars lined its edges. People streamed from the cars to make their way down to the side of the grave. One of them was Katy, who had flown back from Phoenix just that morning. Still numb, I tried to greet those I knew, but so many people had come, I could not see them all through the crowd. From my vantage point, though, I could see the barn that belonged to my brother,

George. It sat next to the river down below. George and his wife, Cookie, lived in Snohomish, and they had been steadfast in their support of me throughout my husband's ordeal. They stood with me now, near my sons. Behind me were Reid and Lydia, holding onto each other and onto me, and standing in unity with all of us were Katy and Asemah, along with Azzam.

Now, though, my feet stood close to an open hole in the ground. Clinically I noticed how perfectly dug it was, with sharp corners and straight edges. But emotionally...*that hole is for my Adnan's body! Oh God, no!* I dreaded the moment the hearse would arrive. When it slowly pulled in front of the grave, with Adnan's body inside, I felt sick, unsure if I could face this final moment without faltering.

There was no other choice, and the process began. I was impressed by the dignity and the love shown to Adnan by the Muslim community. They spoke words and prayers with reverence, and they were gentle with his shroud-enfolded body as they carried it to the grave, Azzam among the bearers. Following Islamic convention, there was no casket. Hamudi and Inaz stood on the other side of the yawning hole, urging Azzam to be careful because of his chronic back pain, but Azzam did not step away. After they lowered my husband's body to the sandy floor of the crypt, the sheikh climbed down and tenderly arranged Adnan's body to lay on its side, facing Mecca, the holy city of Islam. It is the direction Muslims face when they pray. The sheikh then stepped back up to the lawn, with the aid of a man's outstretched hand, and began to speak in Arabic. I did not understand the words, but the demeanor of his speech sliced through the numbness to convey reverence to God and submission to His will.

After concrete slabs were placed on a dirt rim a few feet above Adnan's body to create a crypt—giving me the absurd feeling that he would have air and space—several young Muslim men reached for shovels and made ready to scoop soil from the nearby pile.

Suddenly, our usually serene second son shattered the air with his booming voice.

"STOP!"

The motion of the shovels froze in midair, and all eyes were on Tameem. With a solemn face, he reached for one of the shovels, and the young man holding it gave it freely. Tameem flung the first shovelful of dirt over the crypt. Responding to a signal from his brother's eyes, Rasheed climbed to the pile of soil in his dress greens, medals shining in the sun, and with a thunderous-looking face scooped his own shovelfuls onto the crypt. Tameem tried to hand his shovel to Asem, but Asem shook his head at his brother. He had already participated in much of the ritual and did not want to take part in the covering of the crypt. Azzam had helped to carry his brother to the grave, and he stood between Asem and me, frozen to the spot. Tammy reached for the shovel. She did not know if Islam allowed a woman to participate, but she did not care. This was her Baba, and she wielded the shovel with all her love radiating through the handle to the ground that would cover him. When they were done, Rasheed and Tammy handed the shovels to the waiting Muslim men to finish the job, and Tameem and Rasheed stepped to my side, one on each arm, to support my wavering body, to keep me upright as I watched with tight lips, trying to hold back tears that escaped anyway to fall on the ground unheeded. At that moment, I just wanted to fall into the grave and join my husband. The final separation was just too painful to bear.

When the grave was covered, the people began to dissipate, talking in small groups, paying their respects to me and to our sons and families as they departed. Afterward, our extended family gathered at a local restaurant for dinner, putting off going to the empty house for a little while longer. I did not want to leave my husband up in Snohomish, out under the ground, away from all of us who loved him. Surely he should be with us at the restaurant, telling jokes and laughing like he used to do!

The empty house waited, and it was still empty when we opened the door and stepped inside.

Within the next few days, I bought the gravesite next to my husband's. I just couldn't bear the thought of someone else resting beside him on the grassy hill that overlooked the Snohomish Valley.

CHAPTER 2

My Heart

AIMLESSLY WALKING ABOUT THE HOUSE, I stared at the family photographs that adorned the cabinets and walls of the rooms. Adnan's eyes looked at me from the pictures, bringing memories from far back at the beginning, and I remembered his stories about coming to America.

He arrived on the very day that President John F. Kennedy was shot in 1963. After spending a year in Brazil visiting cousins, he flew to Miami, Florida, to travel to the University of Wyoming, where his oldest brother, Nader, was a graduate student. For luggage he had just a small leather duffel bag, with its outer surface smudged and worn. In his pocket he carried a piece of paper with his brother's name, phone number, and the words "Laramie, Wyoming."

Adnan spoke not a word of English. At a café, he showed a waitress a picture of a pig and shook his head as he pointed at it, frowning. She brought him a sandwich of some kind of meat that was not pork, and he opened his hands holding money his Brazilian cousins had given him. The waitress picked out a couple of bills and a few coins, smiled, and nodded toward the sandwich.

After lunch he used pointing and hand signs to find the Greyhound bus station, bought a ticket to Laramie in the same manner as his sandwich, and boarded the bus.

Nader was thoroughly surprised to see Adnan, as he did not know he was coming. But as long as Adnan was there, Nader persuaded him to get a student visa and start college.

In order to learn the English language, Adnan got a job in the student union bussing tables. Several grandmotherly ladies who ran the kitchen helped him out of kindness to learn basic words and phrases, though he spoke with a strong accent in the beginning.

It was there, in the student union, where I first saw him. As I sat alone at a small, round table surrounded by lunchtime chaos, I watched him clean another table from garbage, dirty dishes, and spills. His short-cropped, thick, dark hair; bushy eyebrows; and olive skin suggested that he was from the Mediterranean. His ample belly pushed his shirt buttons apart a bit, but he moved with grace.

It is strange how a fleeting thought can cross a mind, take root, and grow in the background. *What if he becomes my husband? Maybe he would not care if I ate extra ice cream. I wonder...*

I had never been allowed to date boys before college, and though I had lived all my life near Seattle, my parents wanted me to attend the University of Wyoming, where my stepsister's husband was a professor of mathematics. I suspected it was to keep me under their control. But my wings were spread as I stood on the edge of the nest and looked out to the universe.

A few days after I had seen him from my lunch table, I watched Adnan enter my calculus classroom. The teacher was not there yet, and Adnan used chalk to scribble unfamiliar lettering on the blackboard. Three or four students in the back of the room broke out in laughter. The writing was Arabic, but I never did know what the words said that had evoked the hilarity among his Arab friends, and he left quickly before the professor arrived.

After the class, he met me at the door with halting English.

"Want Coke with me?"

"What?" I said, not sure of what he was asking.

He was staring intently as he smiled. "Coke? Union?"

I don't know why I accepted, but he seemed interesting and I walked with him to the student union. Thelma, one of the older ladies, served us both glasses of Coca-Cola and set a plate of donuts in front of us. Later Adnan told me she had said that, as a couple, our personalities fit together like "a good pair of shoes!"

I fell in love with him on our first official date later that week. He had invited me to an elegant affair, and I wore a pink dress. The occasion involved a dinner and an international film, with an hour to socialize beforehand. I felt socially inept, having had no experience in the dating world. But I tried to smile and act confident.

A short, stout man with crew cut hair and horn-rimmed glasses approached from the center of the crowded room.

"I like your dress," said the man. "In my country, if someone says they like something, you have to give it to him."

I stood there, unsure how to respond. Adnan stepped in front of me, straightened his height, and said, "Is why you no tie, Hamsi?"

With that, he took my arm and led me to another corner of the room, protecting me from social assaults of any type. Yes...that is when I knew. I would love him forever. From that moment, he was my fairy tale prince.

A couple of weeks later, he drove me to Denver, so I could buy a prom dress from a big city shop. On the way back to Laramie, he asked me to "go steady." But his accent and wording made his question hard to understand, and I thought he was asking me to marry him! I said, "Yes!"

Only nineteen, I was considered an underage girl by the state of Wyoming, and I had to have written permission from my father to get married, but my dad sent the letter with an admonition for my soon-to-be husband to be aware of my "spontaneous enthusiasm for just about anything."

Three months later we committed ourselves to each other before a judge in the First National Bank of Laramie, Wyoming. It was semester break. None of our family members could attend, as they were all too far away, and the date had been too sudden for them to plan a trip.

Adnan finished out the spring semester, while I got a job at the university library. My paycheck could not cover tuition and living expenses, though, so we moved to Seattle where my parents had a small farm in a rural area outside the city. Boeing was hiring, and Adnan started working as a junior engineer within days of our move.

Almost four years after our wedding, I woke Adnan up at two o'clock in the morning to tell him I was in labor with our first child. Neither of us knew what to expect, but my water had broken, so we piled in the car to rush to the hospital. On the way, Adnan blew through a red light, but I didn't care. Four hours later, Asem was born. Adnan went back to his Boeing job, a pink layoff slip waiting for him. On that same day, though, he was rehired in a different Boeing position that paid more money.

But that was not to last either. We fell into the bin of the big Boeing layoff in 1971. During that crisis, someone posted a sign by the freeway that said, "Will the last person leaving Seattle please turn off the lights?" A massive number of engineers and technical workers left the region hunting for work elsewhere, and we decided it was time to return to Laramie to finish Adnan's education.

A week before Adnan's graduation from the School of Civil Engineering, Tameem was born in Laramie's small hospital. Only two babies were in the nursery, and I knew which was Tameem when I heard them crying. The little girl's high-pitched "waaa waaa waaa" was silenced by Tameem's low baby voice bellowing out a loud "Waa!" (That moment from the past came back to my mind when Tameem stopped the covering of Adnan's grave with his commanding voice.)

After graduation Adnan tried to find a position as a civil engineer in the Rocky Mountain area, but it was Boeing that wanted him back again, and we moved to Seattle once more, this time to stay.

When Asem was eight, he joined the Cub Scouts. Adnan and I both joined the Boy Scouts of America to help wherever we could, and our circle of friends expanded with the years of service.

Seven years after Tameem's birth, our youngest son, Rasheed, was born. As the boys grew, they all went through the scouting program to become Eagle Scouts. Each developed his own interests, with music or sports, but scouting provided the outdoor adventure that appealed to me, and it was because of a Boy Scout leadership course that I became enamored with the wilderness. My first backpack trip opened a door to a new passion that would stay with me the rest of my life.

Some of the scout mothers wanted to backpack the trails that crisscrossed the Washington Cascades. I joined the group to camp, hike, and even climb volcanoes with them in multiday excursions. One of the women was a mountain guide, and she coached those of us without experience on how to use an ice ax, how to use a climbing rope to walk over glaciers, and other climbing skills.

Once, when I came back from a climb, Adnan was in a sour mood. His mother had come to visit, and though he adored her, he was not happy that I had been gallivanting in the mountains when she arrived.

Our disagreement exploded further when we began to talk about religion. I could not match his devotion to Islam, other than to proclaim that I believed in God with all my heart. Adnan wanted me to convert and practice all the rituals, but I could not follow what I did not understand, and we entered a dark time in our lives.

As time went on, though, we kept our communication open and began to accept each other "as is," he always hoping that I might eventually see his deep beliefs as true.

In my new excitement for the outdoors, I attended a slide show about the Pacific Crest Trail, or PCT, as many call it. The 2,650-mile trail winds through the mountains of California, Oregon, and Washington, all the way from the border with Mexico to the border with Canada. I planned to hike the Washington portion, sometimes with friends, sometimes with my sister-in-law Cookie, and most of it with Adnan, who wanted to join me. His pack was heavy, but his love of the outdoors was similar to mine, so we found common ground where we could grow closer together.

One beautiful evening, after a long day of hiking, we set up camp and sat together on a rocky slope to watch a glorious sunset.

"This is so beautiful!" I said.

Adnan said nothing but kept his face toward the west with a grim look. After a few moments, though, he looked down at my face, which was resting on his shoulder.

"I just wish…I wish you could see my way and practice Islam with me like my mom and sisters," he said.

My heart fell. I loved him so much, but did he not understand?

We slept in silence that night, Adnan grieving that I did not see his way completely, and I grieving that our relationship was tainted by our differing views.

Our friend Joan was with us on this trip but had not seen our troubled interaction.

"Let's get moving!" she said as she shouldered her pack in the morning.

Adnan and I were ready and followed her through a band of tall trees. She outpaced us so was not around to witness an event that changed our relationship forever.

Adnan feared slopes of snow, and a steep one loomed ahead that we had to cross. Joan's steps showed the way.

In those days, I used an ice ax like a cane. Adnan did not have one, nor did he know how to use one, but he had a stout stick in his right hand as he shakily stepped onto the snow.

Something told me to get close, though I had been lagging behind all morning so as not to feel the disapproval emanating from Adnan's being. Steeply below, a pile of jagged rocks poked through the snow at the base of the snowfield.

Adnan slipped. As if in slow motion, I watched him waver and begin to slide, and I heard his walking stick clatter its way to the rock pile. Without thinking, I reached out to grab his pack with my left hand and fell with him while I slammed the pick of my ice ax into the slope with my right hand. The scream of metal slicing icy snow came to a stop several feet below the trail.

Holding the embedded ax for support, I kicked a flat spot into the snow for Adnan to brace his feet. Little by little, kicked step by kicked step, we climbed back to the trail and made it across to bare ground.

He hugged me so tight that I felt like I might burst.

"I love you!" he said over and over.

From that moment he seemed to forget our differences and embrace me for who I was.

Adnan's arthritic knees stopped him from hiking with me after a few years, but he supported me as I hiked the rest of the PCT from the border with

Mexico to the Columbia River, in long sections. He put on a huge party for me when I completed it, out on our big front lawn.

As we grew older, when I was not out hiking, we spent many hours together in the garden or in the house that we had bought and rebuilt to make our own. Even in his seventies, he would come up behind me when my hands were in sudsy dishwater, and he would kiss the back of my neck and dart backward in case I turned to reciprocate with splashing. His eyes twinkled, and he teased me without end, laughing that I could not return his kiss without drying my hands.

"Ya Albe," he called me. (Arabic for "my heart.")

My heart.

CHAPTER 3

The Plan

ADNAN'S CANCER DEMANDED TREMENDOUS ENERGY from me as his caregiver. Once, before he died, I went into the kitchen for a break. Asem was waiting for me there.

"Mama," he said. "You need to have a plan. This is what I tell my patients' families, those who are losing a loved one. You need a plan for afterward, something you can do without thinking, so that you can put one foot in front of another and keep going while you go through the grief process."

I thought about the PCT, with its high mountain passes, often blanketed with snow, the desert terrain in southern California, swift streams, peaceful meadows, and deep forests. Sometimes a hiker is out on the trail without any signs of civilization for a week at a time, and other times the trail passes through towns on roads. The trail is home to deer, bear, mountain lions, and marmots, along with other wildlife of varying sorts. A backpacker on the PCT carries in a pack everything needed for life on the trail, including shelter, sleeping gear, clothing, cook pot and kitchen gear, and hygiene items, among others. Food, water, and fuel are also on the list. But everything needs to be as light as possible, and unnecessary items must be left at home. It is a simple life. As I considered my needs, it seemed a wholesome place to heal, for walking through grief.

I looked into Asem's serious eyes and said, "I think I need the trail."

Because I had already hiked the whole trail in long sections, I knew the beauty and the hardships it would bring. What I didn't know was if I could prepare in time for the annual PCT Kick Off, a gathering of long distance hikers in southern California at the end of April, at Lake Morena, twenty miles north of the Mexican border. Friends who wished me well and wanted to comfort me in some way would be in attendance. There would also be the new crop of thru-hikers (hikers who intended to hike the whole trail in one season) who participated in the gathering for information on trail conditions, water availability, and general hiking advice from veteran PCT hikers. If my husband continued to live, I would not go. But his health was deteriorating too fast to expect that. Not knowing how long he would be with me, I told him I would be back on the trail and think of him whenever I got to a ridge with cell service where I might have been able to call him, as I had done during the section hikes when he remained at home to support me. He just smiled, and I knew he supported the idea.

I would have no time to actually research the trail and prepare a plan for where I might send resupply boxes filled with food and sundry items such as toilet paper, hand sanitizer, and new socks. But I had already done that a few years before when I spent a winter dreaming of thru-hiking the PCT. I seemed to remember printing out the plan and stowing it in my backpack closet, where I kept my gear. During one of my husband's frequent naps, I went upstairs into my bedroom and opened the folding door to that closet. What a mess! Piles of clothing and gear had been hastily stashed to get them out of the way, back when I had returned from another long trail just before Adnan's diagnosis. A cardboard box filled with small items seemed the likely place. Reaching under the pile, my fingers found a few pages stapled together, and there was the plan. A quick scan gave me assurance that it would do, if needed.

The next day I applied for a thru-hiking permit from the Pacific Crest Trail Association. It required that I hike at least five hundred miles. Well, that was only about a fifth of the trail, and I could do that even if I didn't start for several months. I also sent for a "Canada Entry Permit" in case I was able to do all 2,650 miles of it. I felt guilty preparing for the trail while Adnan still lived. But permits took time, and time would be too short if I waited.

Back in the fall, when I had returned from hiking the John Muir Trail in the Sierra Mountains of California to find Adnan so ill, I had stacked unused backpack food in boxes against the wall just outside my kitchen. I should have put the food in the freezer for the winter, but the cancer diagnosis trumped any good intentions I may have had. Now, as I looked at the food, I realized it would have to be trashed, because the ingredients might not be safe to eat, having spent the winter in warm air. So, on the Internet, I ordered new freeze-dried ingredients—beef crumbles, chopped chicken, and vegetables—the main ingredients for when I was ready to assemble the several months' worth of meals, only needing to be rehydrated on the trail.

About the trail, though, I was not as enthused as I would have been under normal circumstances. Even in my childhood, the outdoors had been comforting to my soul whenever my heart was troubled. I looked to the trail this time as a way to walk through the coming grief, to clear my head and help me see the direction I should take…after…

After? I would not hike any trail ever again if only his cancer would just disappear!

My logical mind told me this pronouncement was the "bargaining" phase of grief. Even before Adnan's last breath, the grief process was at work.

"Denial" was the most prominent stage right now. *(Wouldn't he always be with me?)* I could not believe we were actually coming down to the point of death.

"Anger" was the next phase, but so far I didn't seem to be angry. Not yet, anyway.

"Sadness" came and went, but denial shoved it behind a curtain of doubt.

"Acceptance" was not possible. Yes, until it really happened, I would deny that he was dying! With the permits on the way, though, and a written plan from the past on the desk near the kitchen, I could shove "the plan" to the back shelves of my brain and focus on my husband's last days, comforting him, trying to make him well as best I could…and trying to cope with the coming loss.

Of course, a flurry of activity unrelated to my plan followed his death. There was the burial and memorial service, first. Then came the scramble to notify the pension and social security offices. Bills needed to be switched from Adnan's name to mine, as well as the titles for the four vehicles in my driveway, two of which I could not drive because they were standard-shift trucks.

Old memories flooded my head as I waded through the paperwork. Once, long ago, Adnan had tried to teach me how to drive one of the trucks. When to use the clutch was a mystery to me. So was the shifting of a manual transmission. But I did my best. Following his instructions, I found myself zipping along the freeway at the wheel of the truck.

"Don't do that!" he exclaimed with an alarmed voice. "You'll break the engine!"

I took both feet off the pedals and allowed the truck to roll onto the shoulder of the freeway until it lurched to a stop. To this day, I don't know what I did to scare him. But I never tried to learn how to drive a standard shift vehicle again. Now, I owned two of them.

Gradually the paperwork dwindled, and I had a single sheet listing all the companies I might use for the running of my home and life, and their phone numbers and websites, along with my account numbers, usernames, and passwords. I prepared that sheet in case I needed to use my smartphone to pay bills or check on services while I was away from home.

While working on the financial responsibilities, a new role for me, I began dehydrating bananas, onion tops, and broccoli buds. Using old recipe cards, I prepared a new batch of backpack food, which filled large plastic bags on the chairs that surrounded the dining-room table, already covered with labeled stacks of paperwork.

Another memory came unbidden. I pictured Adnan standing behind me, laughing! I had always been after him about his piles of papers on the dining-room table. The table was seldom clear. Most days we had to sweep the piles to one end before I could set it for dinner. Now my stacks were far worse than his had been. At mealtime, I found myself eating while holding a plate in my lap on a recliner to the side. There was literally no room for a place setting, nor was there a chair available. Adnan, in my mind, shook his head and laughed.

"Now you understand!" his ghost chuckled.

"Yes, sweetheart," my mind answered. "I sure do!"

Slowly the household paperwork was filed away and replaced by lists of addresses for resupply boxes, lists of items to buy or gather, and a stack of maps. A former thru-hiker, whose trail name was "Halfmile," had used GPS waypoints to create accurate maps for the whole Pacific Crest Trail. I bought the map set to have hard copies, but I also downloaded his app for my iPhone that could tell me exactly where I was on the trail when the app was opened.

As I looked at all the trail preparations, my already traumatized spirit slumped under the weight of the work required for my plan. I reached out to my friend JoAnn, who lived in California, near Mt. Shasta.

"JoAnn," I lamented over the phone. "I don't know how to get it all done!"

"I will help you," she offered, and the plan became more possible. She drove almost six hundred miles to come help me prepare. During that week, she taped cardboard cartons together while I prepared shipping labels. For hours she highlighted the trail on the maps in brilliant yellow, while I fine-tuned my packing list. With the boxes lined up in order on the living-room couches, we placed assorted items in each, such as toilet paper, first aid supplies, and hand sanitizer.

We took a break one day and drove to the tulip fields in Conway, about fifty miles north of my home. I wanted to treat JoAnn to a special time, since she had been working so hard to help me. Linda, a mutual friend, joined us for the day, which also included a visit to Deception Pass on Whidbey Island and a ferry ride across a finger of Puget Sound. After dining at a waterfront restaurant, we came home to more prep work for the trail.

Without JoAnn I don't think I could have finished in time to attend the PCT Kick Off. But with her help, I closed the door of my house and said good-bye to the flowers in the yard that Adnan and I had tended together. My little home with so many, many memories over forty years was in the hands of God and in the hands of our son Tameem.

JoAnn drove me to the I-5 freeway and we headed south, toward Portland, where Asem had a temporary assignment for his surgical residency. There I would board a plane to Los Angeles after a short visit with my eldest son, the one who had prescribed the plan as a part of my recovery from the wrenching.

Taking the First Steps

CHAPTER 4

First Days

DEEP IN THOUGHT I SAT by the small rounded window looking down at the mountains far below the jet. *Was I running away from the grief process? Or was I boldly stepping into it?* Much of my gear had been mailed ahead to Lydia, who had agreed to take me out to the trail at Warner Springs. A little one-pound pack rested in the overhead bin above my head with the few clothing items I planned to carry. My eyes tried to pick out the ridges where the trail snaked its way north. *Would I make it that far? Would fires stop me during the hot, dry months of late summer? Would I even want to get very far at all?* I had told my family and friends I would walk until I was done walking. It could be Canada, or it could be next week after the Kick Off.

"Would you like anything to drink?" The flight attendant brought me out of my thoughts.

"Water, please," I answered. I would need to be hydrated, especially since the first seven hundred miles of the PCT are mostly desert.

A short train ride from the Los Angeles International Airport brought me to Oceanside, where Rasheed's family resided. Their home was on the grounds of the Marine Corps base of Camp Pendleton. At the train depot, Lydia smiled from the driver's seat of her waiting car, while Ina and Desmond screamed their welcome loud enough to hear before the doors opened.

"TATIE!" they yelled in unison. (*Tatie* means "grandma" in Arabic.)

"Ina! Desmond!" I enthusiastically called back. The love of grandchildren was medicine for my soul.

After a couple of days basking in their affection, the time came for me to start walking. Lydia and the kids drove me to Warner Springs, where I planned to walk south to the Kick Off. From there I intended to find a ride north to my start point and resume the trail toward the direction of Canada.

Ina and Desmond wanted to watch me take the first steps on the trail, so with the loaded pack on my back, I strode out with a big smile and a cheery wave, which were answered in kind by frantic waving from the back seat as Lydia drove away. Something seemed wrong though.

Under the shade of an oak tree, the sound of rustling paper invaded the silence of the deserted trail as I unfolded the map and slipped reading glasses over my nose. Yes. That's what it was! I had started walking north, not south. Sheepishly, I turned back to the place where the trail crossed the road and began anew, in the right direction.

Slowly, little by little, trail memories from the past began to arise, mixed with the memories of my husband, ill and healthy. Past and present melded together. Thoughts tumbled around, up and down, back and forth, like clothes in a washing machine. As the blue shirt is on top and then sinks while the red shirt bubbles up from underneath, my thoughts rose and sank in the agitation of my mind.

My head had churned a myriad of thoughts by the time I reached Barrel Springs, where the lateness prompted me to stay for the night. There I met "Coach," "First Class," "Double Cross," and "Far Out." On the trail many hikers have trail names, usually given to them by other hikers, but not always. Mine was "Blue Butterfly." When asked I told people my trail name came partly from some of the staff at the high school where I used to work (because of my lighthearted way of working with people there, and because some butterflies migrate from south to north, as I planned to do on the trail). Some of my hiking friends agreed that "butterfly" was appropriate due to my flitting from one side of the trail to the other as I hiked (to see everything I could). I added the word "blue" myself because I loved those little blue butterflies that hang around the mud bogs.

Before turning in for the night, I sent an "I'm okay" message to friends and family via my SPOT Messenger, a small GPS-enabled device that can send a preset message to a group of e-mail addresses but could also summon a helicopter if rescue was needed. I hoped with all my heart I would never need that SOS button. The SPOT routine became a nightly ritual, though, to keep worry away from my sons.

My tent was made of Cuben Fiber, one of the lightest materials used for making shelters. It took up little space, and setup was easy with one trekking pole and several guy lines held out by titanium stakes, their heads painted florescent orange for visibility in the darkness, especially in case one is dropped in the early morning hours before the sun is up. Mosquito netting kept the bugs out. The shelter weighed about a half pound with stakes and guy lines, which made my back happy.

The first night out, sleep came in snatches for me. At the break of dawn, when the sky lightened enough for the stars to fade, I rose to stuff my sleeping bag into the bottom of my pack. Instant coffee of the Starbucks brand "Via" filled my cold Gatorade bottle, which was my main water container for drinking. I carried two one-liter plastic water bladders as well, and because water is heavy, they sat in a front pouch snapped to the hip belt of my pack, thus balancing the weight over my hips.

With a nutrition bar in hand, I left the still-sleeping group of thru-hikers, my shoes crunching on the grit of the trail. Hiking boots are too heavy for my liking, so I use sneakers for long-distance treks. But they have to be a size larger than my normal shoe size. The heat of the desert and the hours of hiking make my feet swell, and too small of a shoe would cause blisters and blackened toenails. My feet do not like to be bound tightly by laces, either. I keep the laces loose enough to make the shoes feel like bedroom slippers. If a little pebble finds its way inside, it's easy to slip off the shoe, dump it, and slip it back on without having to sit down.

The sun radiated waves of warmth most of the day, but clouds puffed up here and there to gather late in the afternoon and darken the tops of the mountains. Thunder broke the silent reverie of my mind, and I actively began to look for a campsite. A saddle of ground between two hills, both laden with dark clouds moving together, looked like it would be my home for the second night of the hike. I flung my pack on the ground, snatched the tent from its stuff sack, and spread it on the flattest spot of the saddle. After quickly unzipping the tent door, I threw the pack inside before setting up the shelter, just in case. Lightning flashes, immediately followed by thunderclaps, drove me to hurry. I did not want to get wet!

Pole in place, guy lines set, tent fabric stretched tight—I dove into the shelter just in time for the first big rain drops to fall. The storm rode over the sky above, boiling clouds fighting with each other, with lightning-bolt swords, crashing and booming, sending rain and hail straight down with deafening noise. As the electric storm dissipated, and the sound of rain subsided, the sun cautiously peeked under the cloud drape to shine golden light on the saddle where I sheltered. By morning the ground was dry and so was I.

My muscles complained this morning. They had not had time yet to strengthen and grow to thru-hiker capacity. This was the day to walk through a garden of blooming barrel cacti, and their beauty brought out my iPhone with its good camera to record and document the landscape. I remembered standing with friends when we came through here in the past, each of us calling our husbands on cell phones from a high point. How I wished to call Adnan again and describe the beauty around me! He must be at home, like before, awaiting my frequent calls just to hear his voice and tell him I missed him! *Oh yes, I miss him!* But he could not answer a call from me anymore. Happiness here surrounded in beauty was mixed with the sadness of permanent separation from my sweet husband, and my feet walked the trail, one foot in front of the other, to bring me down to Scissors Crossing, a junction with a well-traveled road to the town of Julian, California, famous for its pies. *Pie!* How lovely is the sound of that word when one has been eating dehydrated food, even for just a couple of days.

At Scissors Crossing a good-sized bridge provided shade for weary hikers, and several of them were there now, occupying rocks or sitting cross-legged in the dirt. Muffled happy chatter gurgled out from under the bridge, and calls of welcome greeted me as I climbed down a dusty slope to join the others. There was a cooler full of cold drinks, soft drinks as well as beer. I did not drink alcohol, though. Early in the trip, I had decided to live my life as I had when Adnan had been alive. I would not drink alcohol, nor eat pork, but I also would not pass judgment over others who did.

"Anyone need a ride to Julian?" Walking up and calling out was a man by the trail name of "Rock Ocean," who had been transporting hikers to and from town for several days. He was what is called a "trail angel," a person who helps hikers with transportation and sometimes even lodging, meals, or holding resupply packages. Several hikers answered his query in the affirmative. Another trail angel, "Houdini," was also giving rides, and between the two of them, most of us got to have pie in Julian.

My tummy satisfied, I headed back out on the hot and dusty trail that wound steeply up and down through sticker bushes and weeds, little seed pods grabbing at my socks and hitching a ride, poking through to irritate the tender skin underneath. On one hot hill, my pace was slow but steady. Part way up I encountered a man sitting in the sun, directly in the path. A huge, cumbersome-looking pack sat next to him. He had been going downhill, but was too exhausted to keep going, though a cool, shady grove of trees (that I had left not ten minutes before) nestled within our view at the bottom of the hill.

"I am carrying way too much!" he said, his voice laden with misery.

"When you get to Scissors Crossing, you can go into Julian and send home things you don't really need," I suggested.

"I don't have a home anymore," he countered, and he proceeded to give me a history of his recent divorce. I could not help him any other way except to encourage him to lighten his load and to take his rests in the limited shade if he could.

My camp that night was at a high point on the trail, with giant boulders standing guard.

"Did you know you set up your tent next to an ant hill?" Another hiker brought my attention to scampering ants that were the same color as the ground-up grit on which I had set up my shelter. They were so small that I could not see them without my reading glasses. Young eyes, however, could. I left my tent in place due to lack of space, but later, under the light of a headlamp, I watched the ants slow their frantic activity and finally crawl underground for the night, and I snuggled into my sleeping bag watching the stars and a beautiful full moon through the bug netting. Sleep came easily that night. In the morning I carefully packed my gear, trying not to upset the little ants. I had no riders that I could see (even with reading glasses) as I set out on the trail.

Pioneer Mail, a picnic area near the Sunrise Highway in southern California, had a nice surprise as the trail reached the spot. Besides a cool, refreshing water cache for hikers, there was a restroom and picnic tables in the shade. *Woo-hoo!* This called for a long rest to visit with other hikers also attracted to the comforts of the restful place. If I was to make the Kick Off in time, though, I couldn't linger too long. And that evening I found myself at the Mt. Laguna Lodge, where I stayed for two nights, realizing that I had had enough time after all.

The day between those nights, I had my first "zero day" of the hike—a day with no miles logged. Sometimes these days are filled with activities such as grocery shopping, doing laundry, and writing journal posts on the Internet. This zero day was restful for me, however, with no Internet access and only one little store. But I learned that the small freezer shelf in the top of a motel refrigerator is not always cold enough for ice cream. The frozen treat I had hoped to enjoy became a gloppy mess to be washed down the sink.

Though the ice cream had warmed and melted, the windy air outside had chilled during the night. When I left Mt. Laguna, I needed to wear a jacket until the sun rose higher in the sky to warm the air once again.

One foot in front of the other, I walked and walked, memories of my husband coming and going in waves, like the fluttering grasses and tiny flowers that bobbed at the edges of the trail. *Oh, if I could just call him and talk a bit!* Suddenly my wary mind pushed the past away as I watched a man in conversation with a thru-hiker ahead on the trail. It was where the trail crossed Kitchen Creek Road, and the man stood near a parked SUV as he waved good-bye to the thru-hiker and greeted me. The car was metallic blue, dulled by caked dirt. The man seemed friendly, but when he said he was going to get his pack from the car and hike the direction I was going, my gut sent me an alert. I was a woman alone, and into my thoughts burst visions of the Green River Killer, a serial killer who dumped the bodies of his victims in a river south of Seattle until he was finally captured and the killings stopped. The man gave me a creepy feeling, so when I got around a corner, I ran for all I was worth for ten or fifteen minutes, until I came to other hikers and felt safe.

"Hi!" I gasped out, heart pumping, unable to hide the relief in my voice.

"You okay?" one of them asked.

"Oh yes!" I answered. "Have fun!" I called back as I kept going to put more distance between the imagined killer and myself.

A flat area close to Boulder Oaks

When I got to Boulder Oaks Campground, though, another car occupied a parking spot, and familiar, friendly faces greeted me.

"Yogi!" I shouted.

"Blue Butterfly!" answered Yogi, and she engulfed me in a warmhearted hug. Yogi is a legend of the PCT. She had hiked it several times and had put together a handbook with pages describing the many towns along the way and their available resources. She had included phone numbers and directions, as well as recommendations from other hikers of the recent past. I had met Yogi before at hiker gatherings, and she knew of my loss. With her was a friend by the name of "Jackalope," who was accompanied by her young son.

"You must be 'Bear Bait,'" I said to the small boy with long yellow hair. "You are the six-year-old boy I have heard about."

"Six and a half!" he growled at me with a frown.

"Oh, I am sorry!" I replied with seriousness. "Six and *a half,* I should have said."

With that he jumped to the side of the empty fire pit to beat the ground with a stick, my faux pas forgotten in his exuberance.

I would see them again at the Kick Off, just a few short miles away. Registration was scheduled for the next day.

CHAPTER 5

Kick Off

IN THE DISTANCE I COULD see what looked like a dry lakebed. *Could Lake Morena actually be dry?* My questioning mind could not believe how little water was out there this year. After three years of drought, the toll on California's water supply was showing. But as I got closer, I realized there was still some water in the deeper end of the lake, and the campground appeared to be buzzing with activity. I had heard that the organizers of the Kick Off expected about a thousand people, if everyone showed up. I was registered, so there would be a spot for me.

I remembered the guilt I had felt when I sent my registration form to the ADZPCTKO (Annual Day Zero Pacific Crest Trail Kick Off) address listed on the website. Adnan was still alive, and here I was applying for a thru-hiker permit and registering for the Kick Off as if nothing was wrong at home. Something in me stood up and beat back that thought. *You had to prepare for your life after—to get the plan set*, it said to quell the guilt that bubbled up in that washing-machine mind. The guilt slid back under the mass of thoughts, and my feet kept walking until I reached the campground and my eyes lit on a pair of older men sitting at a picnic table, watching as I approached.

The long white hair and beard told me immediately who one of them was. "Billy Goat," another PCT legend and a friend to me, rose and welcomed me to his table to talk a bit before I found my spot to settle.

"How are you doing?" he asked. "Really, how are you?"

We had talked over the phone from time to time during Adnan's illness, and also after he died. Tears welled up in my eyes as I thought, *I don't know how to live without him.*

"I'm doing okay," I said instead. "Day by day, I just keep going. I'll be okay."

Billy Goat looked at me with warm and caring eyes that seemed as if he could see right through any protective screens my spirit constructed.

After I had found my spot and set up my tent among other 2014 thru-hiker camps, I was walking around looking for others I might know and noticed an older man beckoning me to come up to his campfire. It was the campfire of "Honey" and "Bear," who ran a hostel in Maine for Appalachian Trail (AT for short) hikers. It seemed a popular place. Most at that fire were AT hikers who aspired to hike the PCT this year.

"Billy Goat gave us a little of your history," said Bear kindly. "We are sorry for your loss. Both of us have been through it before. Honey lost her husband, and I lost my wife a number of years ago. We understand."

"We were married for forty-eight years," my voice cracked. "It was a fairy tale marriage, really. We loved each other as much when he died as when we met...more so, even, because it was so deep."

As my tears fell, others around who had heard sympathized, but Bear reached out for my hand and squeezed it. At that moment I felt such comfort that I spent most of the rest of the Kick Off at their campfire, neglecting the informational meetings, though I still searched for other familiar faces at times to give them my well-wishes for the 2014 hiking season. There were so many here whom I knew from past years.

Once the festivities of the Kick Off died down and most of us were tucked in for the night, Mother Nature delivered an unexpected surprise. Clouds blew in and heavy rain drenched the campground, almost flooding out some of the campsites. Wind whipped the branches of the trees and drove the rain sideways into tents and shelters. Stakes pulled out of the soggy ground and some of the shelters collapsed, sending their occupants to the restroom area or any other covered building. Many had no sleep that night. My own tent stayed up, but water still splashed in and got my down sleeping bag wet. I joined many others in the vendor area the next morning to buy new, more weatherproof shelters. The storm had been good for the vendors at least! But it was a good lesson for many of us as well. Gear that failed in a storm could end a thru-hike prematurely, and no one wanted that.

My newly purchased tent, though a bit larger than the one I had brought with me, was still less than a pound because of the Cuben Fiber material, but it also would protect me in storms much better. A station near the registration area provided postal service to mail home gear that had been replaced during the vendor frenzy.

The dining area of the Kick Off

One morning of the Kick Off, I got up early, cinched down my pack with lunch, water, and a few items for a day hike, and walked to the entrance road for the campground. Cars were lining up to take hikers to the border with Mexico, so they could slack pack (hike with little or no gear, leaving the overnight gear behind) the first twenty miles from the southern terminus of the PCT to Lake Morena. Soon I found myself at the monument, and after photos were taken of each hiker or group of hikers by all their various cameras, my feet took their first steps north from the border. Having done that section twice before, it was familiar and comforting to just walk. At times other hikers passed me, most being much faster than my sixty-seven-year-old legs could go.

"Blue Butterfly!" a cheerful voice called from behind. "I wondered if I might see you!"

"Oh, wow!" I answered. "'Not-a-Chance?' I didn't know you were out here!"

Her smile beamed back at me, and we chattered happily about old times for a minute, and then she was gone around a bend.

How wonderful! People I had not expected to see just seemed to turn up. And every one of them gave me a boost in spirit.

On the sunny morning that the Kick Off concluded, I carried my gear back to the entrance road where I had arranged with others to meet for a ride to Warner Springs. Waving to others as we drove out of the campground, I reflected on the comfort I had received. I had thought I might go home after the Kick Off, but I was not ready for that yet. My good friend Ann (trail name "Guardian Angel") planned to meet me at Warner Springs and join me for a few hundred miles. Our driver, "Spider Legs," reminisced about the trail during the ride northward, with a slight detour to Julian for another piece of pie. A couple of the passengers were new to the PCT and long-distance hiking, but we all melded together in a common goal—to hike on the PCT or, as Spider Legs could do, to support others on it.

Joined by a Friend for Three Hundred Miles

CHAPTER 6
Joy

ANN STOOD NEAR THE DOOR of the community center at Warner Springs, a big smile on her face.

"Hi, Lindy!" her delighted voice rang out.

I grinned and approached her for a warm hug. Though we had hiked long sections of the PCT together in the past, we had actually met several years prior through a group of friends who called themselves the Mountain Sisters in the state of Washington. Our friendship was not made just of shared hiking adventures; it also relied on a solid foundation of our social gatherings as a collection of strong women with different interests and abilities, some of which included mountain adventures, but many of which also included needlework, travel, books, music, skiing, or just drinking tea while discussing the antics of grandchildren.

Ann's fully loaded pack looked like a daypack. I never have been able to get the weight of my pack down as light as hers. Though mine was smaller than many, it stood several inches thicker and higher than hers against the picnic table on the gravel at the side of the community building.

The miles flew by as Ann and I chattered our way north. Sometimes it felt as if Adnan must be waiting at home as in times past. Other times I felt off, struggled to be organized, like nothing seemed smooth. One such day we hiked in silence, as I could not keep up with Ann that day. My thoughts circled around in my mind, looking for a place to settle—and finally the reason for my coming out to the trail found words among the circling. In my journal I wrote these words at lunchtime:

The trail is a great teacher. Life is like the trail. When you lose someone you love, you are sad and you remember your dear one, but you still must shoulder your pack and go on, one foot in front of the other, step by step, hour by hour. There is beauty along the way, and challenges as well, and your loved one enters your thoughts as you go, but the trail keeps going, and day by day, your life journey continues.

The trail became hard. Energy lagged. Coming down from the San Jacintos, on rocky trail that wound through rattlesnake-infested boulders, I moved ahead of Ann. Downhill was easier for me than for her. Heat radiated off the rocks and beat down on our silver-colored umbrellas, which shaded us enough to prevent heat exhaustion as long as we also stayed hydrated with plenty of water. I had very little water left when I reached the final stretch down to a road that came up from Snow Canyon to a water fountain next to the trail.

Suddenly, a famously recognizable yelp shot up to the trail from the vicinity of the water fountain. "Tarzan," a former PCT thru-hiker, had seen me as I descended, and by the looks of it he had set up a tarp, in the shade of which rested several current thru-hikers. Coolers with drinks, trays of fresh fruit and vegetables, hummus, and chips sat in the middle of the group. This was "trail magic" at work! Surprise gifts of help popped up unexpectedly along the trail once in a while, and this was one such time that was welcome indeed! Ann and I stayed for a couple of hours, but we had to move on and make room for others.

Shouldering our packs, we walked down the hot road toward a wide, open flatland, spread with a blanket of prickly bushes and sandy patches. To the north we could see the bridge over Interstate Highway 10, the freeway that led to Asem's house in Phoenix. But we couldn't make it as far as the bridge, as we had come a long way that day and our bodies needed rest.

Tarzan's Trail Magic

"There's a good-looking flat spot," Ann pointed out, looking east of the trail. Both of us headed that way, dreaming of settled tents and a nest of restful comfort. We were startled in unison by the form of what looked like a large, dark-colored diamondback snake that lazily stretched across the open area we sought. Its rattles were silent, and the snake did not coil, but we backed away carefully, forgetting to take any photographs, and retraced our steps to the trail. (Later we learned it was a timber rattler.) Wind whipped our faces as we dejectedly moved on, ever looking for a likely spot to camp. When we saw a dirt road crossing the trail, we found a flat spot devoid of rattlesnakes, though it was full of stickers and small cacti.

There was a bigger problem, though. It was incredibly windy. Every time Ann got her tent part way up, a gust flattened it. Mine was up and I went to help Ann, but I had no better luck—and the wind seemed to laugh at us as it blew my tent down onto the sand as well. If the wind had been coming from one direction, we might have managed. But gusts changed directions repeatedly, first from one side and then from any of the other sides—never the same.

"What are we going to do?" Ann asked in a frustrated cry. "We can't go on! It's getting dark!"

Looking at the floundering Cuben Fiber and tent netting that seemed to be trying to squirm away through the bushes, I thought of an idea. There would be no rain tonight, and I didn't want snakes or scorpions to be able to slither or scamper around my face, but zipped inside of the un-put-up tent, I could still be protected and my body would hold the tent down in the wind. We hit upon this idea with hope for rest this night. My enthusiasm for the trail lagged, though, especially when another problem presented itself. There was a hole in my air mattress. Resigned to a sleepless night, I lay inside the cocoon, and the adrenaline of the day began to ebb. A new idea came to the surface among all the other jumbled thoughts. With a headlamp, I might be able to see the hole and patch it with special tape I had brought for just such a problem.

The tent draped over my head as I knelt on the bottom fabric above the sand. I could feel the grit underneath, but my hands found the headlamp, and light flooded the inside of the cocoon. I had to use reading glasses to see it, but yes, there it was! There was a slit in the air mattress material, just about a quarter inch long. Tape sealed it, and the repair made for a much more comfortable night. Sleep allowed both of us to improve our moods by morning. And the wind had died.

Now the sun, with no breeze to cool our faces, sent heat waves through the air. The cool of the bridge brought welcome relief, but we found more trail magic there too. Bananas, donuts, and cool drinks filled coolers in the shade, and there was a notebook requesting hikers to sign in, thus letting other hikers know who had passed that way and when.

When we hiked that section in 2008, Ann became ill with the heat, and the employee room of a wind farm had saved her with cold water and air conditioning. Today was Sunday, however, and the wind farm would be closed. Armed with that knowledge, we prepared for a long, hot hike up a blind canyon and over toward the Whitewater River.

What is that sign? I wondered. Shortly after leaving the bridge, we came to a road with a printed notice that led us to the place of a new set of trail angels—"Ziggy" and "The Bear." Ziggy told us that it was going to be 105 degrees that day, and she urged us to stay at her place through the daytime heat and start back out in the cool of the evening. Her place reminded me of a beehive. Hikers were everywhere! Some were talking on phones, and others had just had showers or were hanging newly washed clothing on lines. A run was made to a local fast food place to bring back orders of burgers and fries for hungry hikers.

By late afternoon our feet longed to get started again. With little sunlight left, however, we could not make it up to the high point and then switchback down to the river before dark. Once again, as dusk approached, we were looking for flat spots in windy conditions. Few trees grew on the mostly open slopes, but we each found one to use as a possible windbreak. Like the previous night, though, the wind did not allow us to set up our shelters. We used our tents like bivy sacks again, opening our mats and sleeping bags inside, but this time we used our umbrellas to hold the netting off our faces, and the cocoon became more comfortable.

Morning brought a glorious sunrise, but the powerful wind had increased. As Ann tried to pack her gear, her ground cloth escaped and flew through the air toward the high cliff edge. A small bush snagged the ground cloth and held it for her as she sprinted to the edge where it flapped out over the deep valley of the Whitewater far below. Breathing hard with relief, she retrieved the ground cloth and warned me to hold onto my gear as I packed it away.

The hills were full of flowers and fragrance. Sometimes we walked along the tops of ridges looking down to deep valleys, and other times we followed streams or creeks with camps or places to soak weary feet. Mission Creek was one such waterway. The trail crossed it several times before it wound back up into the hilltops. I remembered going through a burned area after Mission Creek in 2008. My thoughts turned inward once again.

On that past hike, my countenance had been sad due to the devastation of a recent fire. Yucca plants were blackened and bent over, their leaves hanging down like limp hair of a keening soul dying in agony. Black and dead, the landscape had invaded my spirit with sadness. I remember being relieved when the walk through the burn ended. On this day my countenance braced for such a depressed feeling, already saddened by my own loss, but now I could see baby yuccas sprouting from the roots of the burned plants. The roots must have survived in order to send out new shoots! Tiny evergreen trees grew from the seeds of the dead ones too. Life was coming back to the ravaged land. Happiness seemed to fill the air instead of sadness, and one of the first lessons of the trail of grief blossomed into my mind, like the new flowers that dotted the open spaces: Life and joy can follow death and sadness. Life goes on. It is not the end of everything! Joy comes back!

CHAPTER 7

The Jolt and the Talisman

ONE EVENING WE SPREAD OUR shelters among a group of thru-hikers camped near a bend in the trail where the bushes gave way to some open, flat spots. As night approached, the stars twinkled overhead and a deep-orange moon rose in the east. Quiet talk and soft laughter ricocheted between the tents and the sleeping bags of cowboy campers (those who slept in the open without shelters). I decided to use my MP3 player for the first time on the trip. Music appealed to me this night. I thought it might help me relax into restful slumber. With anticipation I slithered into my sleeping bag, put the ear buds in place, pressed the "on" button, and closed my eyes. Adnan's voice began to chant from the Koran.

Oh God! My heart leaped with the unexpected jolt! The grief within me tore open and screamed with pain. I tried to be silent as tears welled and ran down the sides of my face, but I could not contain the keening that the shock of hearing my husband's voice evoked. Ann heard my sobbing.

"Lindy, are you okay?" she asked with concern. "What's wrong?"

"Adnan's voice is on my MP3," I said through tears. "I thought I was going to hear music, but his voice came on instead. I miss him so much!"

I had forgotten that he had recorded his voice reading the Koran back in 2008, before I left with Linda and Ann for our first thru-hike attempt. Ann reached out with gentle words, and gradually the shock receded.

Cold and windy, the next morning brought chilly thoughts as well as chilly air. I hugged myself as I began to walk, unable to stay warm in the predawn departure. The newly abraded grief ached in my center, and the world around me seemed colorless.

What am I doing *out here?* My brain demanded answers while I waited for Ann to open a wooden gate that crossed the trail. *Why am I even* out *here?* As these dark thoughts entered my consciousness, I noticed something brushing back and forth above my ankle. It seemed so insistent that my thoughts were broken and my eyes looked down. There, by my feet, whipping in the wind, grew the most beautiful bouquet of yellow wallflowers I had ever seen. Lush with elegance, in perfect symmetry, the flowers seemed to be nudging me with an urgent message: *Yes, you do belong out here! This is where you need to be!*

And I thought clearly of Adnan, that he was speaking through the flowers. It may have been my imagination, or wishful thinking, but I like to believe he was there that morning to encourage me to go on with my plan and stay on the trail…at least for now.

In the nights thereafter, I found I was able to purposely set the MP3 player on his recorded voice. With my eyes closed, I imagined him sitting by my head in the tent, comforting me with his chanting. And as the days went on, a yellow flower of any kind became a talisman to bring my beloved husband to me in memory.

There were many yellow flowers out there as we continued to move north.

CHAPTER 8

The Big Bear Episode

We had heard through the hiker grapevine that the weather was turning, and if we could not get into Big Bear City by the next day, we would most likely encounter snow. My sleeping bag had not kept me warm enough on many nights, so I was concerned. There were several roads that promised a possible hitch into town, but we would not reach any of them this night.

As we approached Coon Creek Camp and a cliff called "The Jump-Off," we heard music coming from a white pickup truck parked on a dirt road at the cliff's edge. The door was wide open, and three young people watched us climb the final steps to the road crossing.

"Are you PCT hikers?" they shouted our way.

"Yes!" we said in unison.

"Want a beer?" They grinned and lifted their own beers in salute, waiting for our answer.

That was the start of an incredible experience. Dylan, Katie, and Jake were cousins, and they had just lost their grandfather the night before. They were coping with his death in their own way—off-roading with plenty of beer—to dull their grief. Katie and Jake were from Idyllwild in southern California and had helped PCT hikers several times in the past. Dylan, who lived alone in Big Bear City, wanted to help hikers too, and he enthusiastically offered to bring us to town to spend the night at his home. At first we resisted, but Dylan looked so hopeful, and the weather forecast nudged us from behind toward their truck. The back seat of the dual cab was quickly emptied, our packs cheerfully hoisted into the truck bed, and we piled in. Neither Ann nor I wanted a beer, but cans were popped open one after the other among our new friends, and talk flowed freely between us.

"We were out here off-roading and stopped to see the view. How 'bout we take you down some bitchin' roads and let you see what we do for fun?" Jake asked hopefully. Laughter bounced around the cab, along with generous phrases that included the words "bitchin'" or "fuckin' bitchin'" spoken with enthusiastic abandon.

What have we gotten ourselves into? I thought with a bit of trepidation. The truck slowly rumbled down the gravel road, lurching as it crawled over boulders and dipped into chuckholes. The narrow road cut across and down a steep slope.

Don't look down, my mind instructed. So I laughed with the others and prayed silently that the wheels would stay on the road.

I thought the adventure was over when the truck jolted to a stop, because our way was blocked by broken chunks of a downed tree. The boys got out of the truck and, grunting with effort, rolled the heavy lengths of wood out of the way, and we were back on course.

Around a bend, a second, larger tree spanned the road at an angle, butting up against a jagged, two-pronged stump. Without hesitation Dylan set his beer can on the passenger seat and hopped out, gravel crunching under his feet.

"This needs a rope!" he shouted back to the truck.

"Bitchin!" said Jake as he stepped out beside his cousin.

Katie retrieved a rope from the truck bed and helped the boys to tie it to the end of the tree that was nearest to the inside edge of the road.

"We can pull that tree to the outside, I think," said Jake.

Behind the steering wheel again, he put the transmission in reverse and stepped on the gas. The truck jumped backward, and the beer can danced in the air, spilling droplets. Jake's hand shot out to catch it before it dumped on the seat.

In one swift motion, he set the brake, swung the door wide, and popped out with the beer can to set it on a rocky cubbyhole in the road bank.

"Can't lose the beer!" he said and vaulted back to the driver's seat.

Again he put the truck in reverse and stomped on the gas pedal. The straining force snapped the rope, making the truck jerk backward.

Jake jumped outside again to confer with Dylan and Katie, while Ann and I watched the entertaining drama from the back seat.

"The log's against that stump, and it's not going anywhere," said Katie.

"Yep," said Jake.

Dylan, not willing to give up just yet, shoved the log with gritted teeth. Jake and Katie tried to help, but the downed tree would not budge.

"That's it," said Jake. "Dylan, I got to back up to a wide spot to turn 'round. Could ya walk behind while I do it?"

"Sure," said Dylan as he snagged his beer from the road bank. He began guiding the truck's backward progress to a place where Jake could jockey it back and forth until it could be turned around.

As we drove past Coon Creek Camp, we could see several small tents dotting the flat area. Our thru-hiker friends were settled in for the night. As for Ann and me, our evening was just beginning.

Twenty-seven-year-old Dylan had short brown hair, dimples, and an engaging smile. His girlfriend, Morgan, slender with long dark hair, came over with a delicious macaroni dish to accompany Dylan's home-cooked meal of chicken, rice, and salad. A neighbor joined us for a night of stories as we sat circling the coffee table in the small living room. Our stories of hiking adventures alternated with their stories of motorcycle racing and off-roading. Laughter kept the grief at bay most of the time.

"Why'd you have to go and say that?" Jake asked leadenly when a story brought their loss heavily down to the front. But soon the laughter started again as new stories covered the old.

It was past midnight by the time we retired to the room where Dylan had spread sleeping bags over bunk-bed mattresses on the floor. The cozy little bed welcomed us to a night of restful sleep.

Morning brought snow to Big Bear City and to the surrounding mountains. Our thoughts turned to the hiking friends out there. While we enjoyed protection from the cold weather, and a chance to wash our clothes and resupply in comfort, they might be shivering, trying to make it to a road with hope that a car would pass by and pick them up. By the end of the day, the snow had stopped and stars came out to sparkle above in a clearing sky. Dylan invited us to stay a second night, and so we did, extending our time in his hospitable home.

The next morning, as promised, Dylan and Morgan drove us back to Coon Creek Campground. After good-bye hugs, we hiked upward, and the little truck winked in and out of the distant trees as it descended through the forest on the dirt road.

Guardian Angel and Blue Butterfly reminisce about the Big Bear
adventure before heading north from the Jump-Off

I reflected on our experience as it pertained to the grieving process. Each of us must find our own way through—Dylan, Jake, and Katie no less than I. The pain of their loss, and mine, will slowly decrease as new stories cover the old, bringing healing laughter and joy. And the memories of our loved ones will mellow and warm our hearts as time goes on, as long as we allow ourselves to feel the losses and to finally let them go.

CHAPTER 9

New Stories

THE NIGHTS BECAME COLD, WHILE the days were still hot. On the day we reached Deep Creek Hot Springs, the heat radiated off the rocks and up through the soles of our hiking shoes. The hot springs was a place where clothing was optional. Tanned bodies adorned the rocks above the creek, and some of them attempted to tightrope walk across the span of water, almost always falling with a splash amid hoots of laughter. Before continuing, Ann and I, fully clothed, dipped our roasted feet in the cool water while we ate lunch. We thought this busy place would be the exciting part of the day, but our trip out brought another new experience for story-making.

The narrow trail climbed along a cliff edge, circling around the ends of the hills in sweeping contours, and dipping in and out of side canyons. Deep Creek cascaded through the valley over rocks, looking like a tiny, winding thread far below, but echoing with sound that filled the air. As we hiked along, a new sound began to cover that of the creek—the thump-thump-thump of a helicopter.

"I wonder if they are chasing the campers out of Deep Creek," I said. It was illegal to camp there, and yet we had seen several tents along the shore. Back in 2008 when I had hiked this part, we heard that the campers had been chased out by helicopter the day after we had actually spent the night under the "No Camping" sign.

"I don't know," answered Ann. "I hope nobody is hurt up there somewhere." The helicopter had been moving back and forth along the trail and even hovered over us for a few minutes. Now it seemed to stay close to one depression of the area ahead of us.

A hiker coming the other way told us that someone had fallen and hit his head. That was all we knew, until we reached the scene. A group of people arguing and a rescue stretcher blocked our way. The bush-covered slope to the right rose steeply, and that on the left dropped precipitously. There was no way for us to go around, so we had to stay and witness the event.

A man with long brown hair and a bloody forehead sat on the stretcher, looking confused, but he got up and staggered in our direction, while another yelled belligerently at the rescuers. A small woman tried to guide the injured man back to the stretcher, but the angry man would not allow it. His sweeping black hair did nothing to obscure the stormy expression on his enraged face.

"It's gonna cost you five hundred dollars if you go in that helicopter, man!" he screamed. "Don't do it!"

"Please," enjoined the woman. "You are hurt! They can help you!"

"No!" the other man yelled. "Five hundred dollars, man!"

The injured hiker lurched toward the others, then turned and teetered back toward Ann and me, and we instinctively stepped backward a few feet. We were afraid that if he fell and grabbed one of us, he would pull us over the cliff edge.

While the hikers were dressed in shorts and light sweatshirts, the rescuers were fully clothed in bodysuits and helmets. It was clear they could not do their work under the circumstances, and they removed themselves back to the hovering helicopter.

The party with the injured hiker hugged each other in a wider part of the trail, swaying and groaning under the seriousness of their situation. Ann and I took the opportunity to slip by and hurry forward. Within a few minutes, a ground crew of rescuers reached us, and we told them all we had seen. They had been in radio contact with the helicopter, so they had come prepared for a confrontation. We did not stay to see it but kept moving to keep pace with the sun as it crossed the sky. We did not want to be out along the cliff in darkness.

That night we camped on a bit of sand and had the company of another hiker who had also been delayed.

"Happy Mother's Day!" he called out in the morning.

Wow! I had forgotten about Mother's Day. At Silverwood Lake that evening, a ranger gave us a campsite for free, with another "Happy Mother's Day" wish. It was a day to talk with the boys by phone, a day to connect with my loved ones back home, and a day for new stories to encroach on the old. Though the old ones were still raw and close to my heart.

CHAPTER 10

A Chance for Rasheed to Help

THE TRAIL IS HARD ON socks. Trail grit eats holes right through them, and socks with holes cause blisters. Blisters are bad news for hikers. When I discovered the holes in my socks, I was not in a place where I could just go to a store and replace them. We were headed toward Cajon Pass, near where the trail crosses Interstate 15 between the San Bernardino Mountains and the San Gabriel Mountains. The main attraction for hikers there is the golden arches of McDonald's, where hikers can refresh after a usually hot, grueling descent. A couple of convenience stores might have socks, but there were no promises. Slowly an idea took shape in my mind.

At home Tameem was checking on my house, watering my plants, and mowing the lawn to make it look like someone still lived there. In Phoenix Asem was using his computer to keep my finances in order so I would not be without money. Rasheed, however, had no way to help me—until now. He and his family lived at Camp Pendleton, about an hour and a half away from Cajon Pass. I called Lydia.

"Sweetheart," I said, "I don't want to impose, so please let me know if you can't do this. Is there any way you could pick up some socks for me from REI and bring them to Cajon Pass? I'm taking a zero day on Tuesday. If you could, I would be forever grateful! My socks are worn out!"

"Sure, Mama!" she answered. "Tell me what kind of socks you need. I'll look them up on the Internet." In minutes she found a picture and sent it to my iPhone for verification. On Tuesday she arrived at the Best Western (where I was staying) with Rasheed and the kids, bearing gifts of socks, fuel, and a fresh water bladder. They also treated Ann and me to a dinner at the Outback in Victorville, a few miles north by freeway.

I felt the love of my boys—all of them—as they and their families did everything they could to make my journey easier.

I would not have to worry about blisters, with new socks cradling my feet. But Ann already had some bad ones.

"Lindy, I'm going to get a ride to Wrightwood and wait for you," she said. "These blisters are killing me!"

She winced as her fingers prodded the angry bubbles on her heels and toes.

"Oh, wow!" I said. "Those look painful!"

"They are!"

The next morning, I set out alone to stop for a quick apple pie breakfast at McDonald's before continuing down the road to the trail. Gravel crunched under my feet as I passed underneath the freeway, the sound partly muffled by the drone of heavy traffic.

I passed a couple of private residences and then began the climb up the hill on the west side of I-15. On the way up, the coolness of the morning gave way to warm sunshine. I stopped in shade a time or two, but the hotel stay and good dinner provided enough energy to keep me going at a good pace most of the way up.

Near the top of the ridge, I picked up a strong odor I had never encountered before.

What is that smell? I thought.

I asked a hiker who caught up to me if she knew what it was.

"That's poodle-dog bush!" she said.

"Where?" I asked.

"There! See the tall fluffy balls over there where the burned trees are? Don't touch them! You'll be sorry!"

Poodle-dog bush

I spent a night on the ridge, but in the morning walked to Inspiration Point, a scenic overlook on the road to Wrightwood. Parked on a patch of gravel was the blue van owned by Rock Ocean, who had ferried me (and others) to Julian for pie. He stood watching me come toward him, arms folded over his chest with a big grin on his young, bearded face. He gave me a ride to Wrightwood, where Ann had secured a hotel room.

After Wrightwood our hike together was plagued by various irritations. Ann's blisters tortured her feet. My feet complained because of road-walk detours. Poodle-dog bush, the plant I had noticed because of its odor, was a new kind of plant that grew in the burned areas of southern California, and it clogged the trail in places, forcing hikers to either take a chance of touching the plant, and thus contracting a painful skin rash worse than that of poison oak, or walk miles on roads.

We were also irritated by too much togetherness. We argued like siblings over silly little things that seemed important at the time but were really too insignificant to remember later. Still, I was sad to say good-bye to Ann when her sister picked her up at Soledad Canyon. She had been with me for three hundred miles. We had laughed and cried together, overcome hardships of the trail as a team, and helped each other to find ways to deal with whatever came up. She had comforted me when grief pulled me down, and I would miss her dearly. I camped with a crowd of thru-hikers in the field of the KOA, a private campground on a busy road in Soledad Canyon. Ann was gone. In the midst of all the hikers, I felt more alone than ever.

Alone on the Trail

CHAPTER 11

Pushing On

As usually happens in any part of life, rest rejuvenates the spirits, and I woke with hope for a good day of solo hiking. A new urgency began to color my plans. I had promised Reid I would be home for Father's Day, and I needed to hike to a place where travel would be easy. Kearsarge Pass in the Sierras had been my planned exit point, but the problems of the last few weeks had slowed my progress and I did not think I could make it that far in time. I was determined to hike longer each day to make it as far as I could.

I traveled ten and a half miles to the Saufley's Hiker Heaven that first day, and twenty-three and a half miles to the Anderson's Casa de Luna the next. Both families are long-time trail angels who boosted my spirits as well as fulfilled my need for a place to stay. They knew of my loss, and their warm, knowing hugs enfolded me in comfort.

Because of a recent fire, I had to walk a long road the third day, for twenty-two miles. Wind whipped dust in my eyes as I plodded along, and my body yearned for the scant shade that trees provided in a few places. The water I carried seemed heavier than usual. The wind grew stronger as I hiked the road over the exposed terrain that approached the turnoff to Hikertown, one of the oddest places on the PCT.

Hikertown is a hostel that sits by itself on a vast, open plain split by the California Aqueduct. I walked through the entrance to Hikertown, a wooden gate that opened on a scene that could have been out of an old Western movie. Small buildings with storefronts marked with signs that said things like "Doctor's Office," "Feed Store," and "Sheriff" lined the dirt road. What looked like a farmhouse sat in the back of a big lawn surrounded by a split-rail fence. Near the house was a building buzzing with hikers.

Terrie Anderson and Blue Butterfly at Casa de Luna

"You can stay in the Doctor's Office," stated the proprietor of the place when I registered. He led me to one of the little buildings that contained a mattress on a metal bedframe and an old wooden dresser…and nothing more. I took a photograph of the building to share with Asem, since he is a doctor. He would chuckle at its quaint appearance.

After lounging with other hikers in the general meeting place of the big side building, we each retired to our respective movie-set buildings. Wind rattled the thin walls of my home for the night as it rushed through the unobstructed desert around Hikertown. But I was protected, and the wind could not get to me, though it tried as hard as it could.

Before dawn I began my trek beside the California Aqueduct in the Mojave Desert, and after three days of hot, windy hiking, my feet touched the road where I could hitch into the town of Mojave. In town I spent some time with an old friend, "Mama Bear," who steered her electric wheelchair beside me on the way to the post office to pick up my resupply box.

A PCT sign beside the California Aqueduct at sunrise, just behind Hikertown

"It is not here," announced the man behind the counter. "I'll look again, but I couldn't find it."

I looked at Mama Bear, who seemed as startled as I was. "You'll find it," she said. "Or you can get what you need at Stater Bros." Stater Bros. was a grocery store at the far northern edge of town.

"It's not here," repeated the postal worker. "Maybe you sent it to your motel?"

I had registered at the Days Inn for a two-night stay, but the box was not there either. Mama Bear had gone home by the time I began my walk to the grocery store. On a whim I stopped by the Motel 6 on the way, and my box was there in the stack behind the counter! I had sent my resupply box to

Motel 6 with the intent to stay there, but I had forgotten. Laughing at myself I resolved to enter the box locations into the "notes" section on my iPhone in the future as I mailed the boxes out. Sheepishly I returned to the Days Inn and called Mama Bear, who laughed with me in relief.

CHAPTER 12

Scary Cows and L-O-V-E

WHILE IN MOJAVE I LOOKED ahead at possible exit points from the trail and made my plans. Several towns where I could catch the Eastern Sierra Transit bus going north were available to me, so I bought my plane ticket home from Reno. Now, with the ticket purchased, I could gauge my progress and move at a pace to meet the deadline. I aimed for Lone Pine, a town at the base of the eastern slopes of the Sierras.

A trail angel by the name of Ted dropped me off on Highway 58 where the trail crossed the road. The baking heat withdrew under gusts of wind but returned each time the wind subsided. It was going to be a hot climb.

Lounging around a small mound by a fence were several young, bearded thru-hikers, laughing and recharging with food and water before heading north on the trail. I greeted them cheerfully, but did not tarry. I needed to make as many miles as possible, and my pace was slow.

One day on that stretch, I had gone over twenty miles, hoping to camp in a spot where I had spent a night with other thrus in 2008. All along the trail were signs stating that, outside the narrow corridor, the land was private. We were not supposed to camp there.

But I was tired! Looking up the hill through a deep forest, I thought I saw the familiar knob. Brush and fallen tree limbs littered the slope, but I crunched and flailed my way upward to find the old flat spots that hid behind a few boulders the size of wheelbarrows. I released the waist belt and dropped my pack, relief at having found my home for the night.

By now I knew the routine: get out the tent and spread it out on the ground, fish in the mesh pocket for the tent stakes, and start the stove so it could heat water for dinner while I put the shelter up. Before I began the nightly pattern, I flung a few of my belongings out on the grass, looking for a jacket to keep the bugs away. And then…I heard it.

"Moooooo." A loud, hoarse bellow echoed through the air.

Oh no! I thought with panic. *Cows!*

I was afraid of cows. They were big and scary. I grabbed the scattered gear and stuffed it in my pack in a whirlwind effort, not bothering to organize any of it, or even get it completely inside. I was out of there! Dangling objects hit my legs as I scrambled back to the trail and started moving. *Did I get it all? Had I left anything back at the rock pile?* I hoped not! I surely did *not* want to go back to where cows filled the forest.

The bellow rang out again, and it was closer. Around the bend of the trail, a bolt of shock struck my heart. There, right in the middle of the trail, stood the biggest black cow I ever saw, and I was frozen to the spot. She looked at me but did not budge. The trail was the only way through the brush and branches that clogged the side slopes. There was no other route. As we stared each other down, a bit of courage welled up, and I took a hesitant step forward. Her eyes widened, and then she turned and bolted down the trail, veered off to the side, and bounded through the scrubby thicket, bawling as she went. When I got to the spot where she had stubbornly stood, I could still hear her complaining in the distance.

That crisis over, I still needed a place to camp. And a few more miles found me at the base of a huge old pine tree, dusk coming on fast. Fallen pine needles had made a soft, flat bed, too thick for tent stakes. Darkness grew as I prepared the tent as a bivouac, and I relaxed under the comfort of the sheltering tree once I was zipped inside the mosquito netting.

In the morning an inventory of my gear found it all present. I packed it together and started the trail before sunrise. The light of dawn, soft on the horizon, was enough for me to see my way. Stepping up to the high point before the trail turned to go down the other side of the ridge, my eyes lit on a small patch of flat sand—too small for a tent, but big enough that someone had written with large letters L-O-V-E in the grit. "Love." What a beautiful word! That word seemed appropriate somehow. It was medicine for a forlorn soul.

A friend once said, "Love is the opposite of fear." Well, I'm glad the lettering in the sand came after the cows. Those letters colored the rest of my day with peace and a bit of joy. I would remember that spot farther on the trail, when my grieving had progressed enough to grasp the meaning—at least what it seemed to mean to me.

CHAPTER 13

The Bashing

THE HIGH DESERT STRETCHED OUT to the north, seemingly endless. Most hikers had to carry extra water through sections like these because so many of us travelled the trail that water caches, collections of bottled water supplied by trail angels and placed in shady spots, were often overwhelmed and empty.

An example of a water cache along the trail, this one just south of Scissors Crossing

As I approached Walker Pass, knowing I couldn't depend on the caches, I made a plan. If a water cache did not exist at the campground, and if there was no water in the cistern the guidebook said was down in the bushes near a bend in the road, then I would hitch into Lake Isabella to get water and spend a night in one of the motels.

Shuffling through dust and heat, I looked down from the trail on Walker Pass, occasional cars rumbling on the winding ribbon of the highway, well below the perch where I walked. A bright blue tarp quivered in the wind near a dirt road. *What could that be?*

Oh yes! It was a weekend! People must have come up from town to camp.

When I reached the side trail that led to the campground, though, a posted sign gave me a surge of hope. "Hiker Trash Wanted!" it said. That could mean only one thing…trail magic!

Trail Magic at Walker Pass

Yogi and some friends, including Jackalope and Bear Bait, had set up a large tarp with picnic tables, chairs, trash cans, kitchen area, and yes... water! PCT hikers sat in a circle of chairs drinking sodas and telling stories. Bear Bait (six *and a half* years old, remember!) met me at the edge of the tarp with a soda, a string of Mardi Gras beads, and a button with his picture on it. After a warm hug from Yogi, I plopped down in a chair and blissfully sagged into it. Within minutes someone handed me a paper plate with a fresh, melted cheese sandwich accompanied by a slice of dill pickle. The unexpected treats worked their magic, and I was content to enjoy it for a while.

Yogi

But I did not want to camp at Walker Pass, so after a dinner of rice and bean burritos, I said good-bye to my trail friends and hiked out of the camp area, crossing the nearly empty highway to ascend back into the mountains to the north.

The trail climbed an open slope with long switchbacks. A few trees inhabited the tops of the ridges, and the upper forests spilled into a dip between two hills, to which I arrived near dark hunting for a camping place. Wind howled through the branches, making it difficult to pitch my tent. I tried several spots before I found the one that seemed to be the best. A few other thru-hikers arrived shortly after I had settled, but they chose to camp without shelters, and low bushes were enough to block the wind from their chosen spots. There might have been as many as eight hikers at the saddle that night.

My tent, hiding from the wind

Before sunrise we all arose and prepared to start the new hiking day. One by one the other hikers left, and I was alone again. And I could not find one of my tent stakes.

I never lose a tent stake! I find other people's tent stakes, but I never lose one of my own! Maybe I dropped it while trying out the other flat spots the night before, when I was trying to find a wind-protected place for my tent.

In the early morning dark, warmly dressed, I shined my headlamp about, looking closely at the ground. I searched, bent over, inching from place to place to try to find the tiny titanium stake, and I rammed my head forcefully into the broken-off end of a pine branch.

"Ouch, that hurt!" I exclaimed to myself, holding my forehead in my hands for a moment to let the pain pass.

I had not yet found the tent stake, so I began my search anew. *Thwak!* Almost immediately my head struck the same pointy branch end, this time with enough impact to bring me to my knees, and I sat down on the rough, curved trunk of a leaning tree, cradling my head.

You must accept *the loss.*

These words seemed to come unbidden into my mind. Again...

You must accept *the loss.*

My brain applied those words to the tent stake, but my heart whispered reference to the loss of my sweet husband.

I sobbed.

"But I don't *want* to accept his loss!" I cried out to God and the heavens. My voice breaking, I pleaded with God to take away the loss—to make it all just a bad dream. I wept, keening my sorrow among the trees on that saddle, until my tears were spent.

I didn't care who might hear me right then, but I was still alone. My heart resigned to the loss, I lifted my eyes to the ground in front of my feet. The stupid tent stake lay in the sand, looking innocent. *This is where you dropped me. It's not my fault,* it seemed to say.

I picked it up and finished packing quietly, reflecting on the experience. It felt like God had allowed me to bash my head in order to get my attention. It seemed like He was telling me, "You are here to grieve! Get on with it!"

Later, when I took off my fleece hat, the place on it where I had bashed my head was dark with congealed blood. My injury would need to be cleaned. I had to do it by feel, with the small square of an alcohol swab taken from the first aid kit in my pack.

The next couple of hours I hiked with a subdued attitude, trying to think just why I had to go through the bashing. *Was it just carelessness? Was it coincidence? Or was it more? I had been enjoying the trail. Had I forgotten the purpose of the trip?* So many questions and random thoughts circulated around the corners and twisting pathways of my brain.

I was still analyzing the morning incident when I reached a likely resting place. The adjacent rocks obscured most of the view, but I noticed I could see a bit of desert through a crack. I sat on a flat boulder and got out my phone so I could open Halfmile's app and see exactly where I was.

*Ring a ling ling...*went the phone with an alert. A voice-mail message had come in. That meant there was phone service here! The message was from my husband's brother, and I touched the "Call Back" button. Azzam, who I had not seen since the memorial service for Adnan, welcomed my call enthusiastically. I blubbered out the story of the bashing, and Azzam comforted me with stories from the old Arab world, and with the first part of the "Serenity Prayer," which he had found on a coin in the road one time and had saved:

God grant me the serenity to accept the things I cannot change, the courage to change the things I can, and the wisdom to know the difference.

Azzam did not know that the prayer—that is, the most used version of the prayer written by Reinhold Niebuhr, an American theologian who passed away in 1971—had been used for years in helping people with addictions or other problems.

Azzam was the one person I really needed at that time. He said all the right things to bring peace back to my soul. I asked him to call my boys to let them know what happened, but I was okay and would call them when I could.

As I climbed ever higher above the desert, more and more of it could be seen. I felt inspired to call the boys myself, but when I attempted to call, there was no cell service. The only cell service had been down in that little cove of trees to the side of the trail where I had rested and found the message from Azzam.

Over the next couple of days, I made it to Kennedy Meadows, the gateway to the High Sierra from the south. While I was walking, my thoughts went back to the lessons of the past few days. The word "love" in the sand kept coming to the front of my mind. And I realized that the love Adnan and I had shared for over forty-eight years could never really end. Love does not die! Adnan's failing body may have died, but his love and his spirit still exist (*present tense!*)...just not on the same plane as mine. These intense thoughts brought a measure of comfort as I hiked through the transition from desert to mountainous terrain, nearing the exit trail I would take to go home for Father's Day.

The beauty of the high desert

Instead of the Joshua trees of the desert, Jeffrey pines and giant sequoias began to populate the more mountainous slopes through which I climbed. The grit of the trail came from ground-up granite, and the fragrance of evergreens filled the air. I had a choice of three different exit trails, all leading down to Horseshoe Meadows, a place where I could get a ride to Lone Pine, a bus from there to Reno, and a plane from Reno to Seattle. I chose the third option so that I would be as far as possible along the trail before descending, thereby being farther along when I returned. I was not ready to end the hike yet. It would be just a pause.

Home and Back

CHAPTER 14
The Father's Day Interlude

FATHER'S DAY FOUND ME HOME again for a couple of weeks. Asem, who was finishing up his Portland surgical rotation, drove up to Seattle in a rental car to be with Tameem and me for the big day—to remember Adnan as well as to celebrate their own fatherhood with loved ones. Extended family and friends filled Tameem's house for a barbeque on Father's Day. Everyone wanted to share remembrances of Adnan and hear stories of the trail, and our gathering went on into late in the night.

At home I frantically spent my time preparing resupply boxes for the rest of the hike from the Sierras northward to Canada. I also had to shop for warmer sleeping gear, as I had already had some cold nights, and past experience told me that I could encounter freezing temperatures in the higher elevations of the Sierras, even in the middle of the summer. Furthermore, my hiking shoes had worn out and needed to be replaced. Altogether it was a daunting task, but I got it done and picked up Asemah from the airport on the last day before leaving home. She flew in from Arizona to ride with me to Portland in Asem's pickup truck, which he had stored in my driveway during his time in that city. The plan was for Asem to use his truck to drive me back to the trailhead at Horseshoe Meadows on his way home to Phoenix.

The night before Asemah and I headed south, we went over to Tameem's house. I brought something for Saphira. At five years old, Saphira had a hard time understanding my long absence, having been so close to us, *Tatie* and *Jido* ("grandmother" and "grandfather" in Arabic). When she used to come over to our house, she wanted to play with a jeweled butterfly that was on our dining-room buffet. Adnan always made her put it back when he found her with it because it was delicate. That last night I brought it to her.

"Keep it for me, sweetheart," I said. "You can see it and remember me, and know that I am being careful. You can give it back when I return from the trail."

Asemah was a fun companion for me in Asem's big truck. Asem had outfitted the truck with a huge gas tank that burned either diesel or vegetable oil. I was not comfortable driving such a large vehicle, but Asemah's happy little voice talking and singing as I drove made my time behind the wheel go fast.

"Look at that, Tatie!" She pointed excitedly toward the "Welcome to Oregon" sign as we crossed the bridge over the Columbia River. Soon she was in her daddy's arms, and before the morning was over, I sat in the passenger seat with Asem at the wheel, helping to navigate our way out of the city.

Once in California we crossed to the east side to drive south on Highway 395. It was late in the day when the truck began to buck and jump, the engine seizing, choking, and coughing. Asem pulled over.

"I think the fuel filters are clogged," he stated with assurance. After resting the truck and following some kind of mechanical procedure involving restarting and revving, the truck drove smoothly until we had to climb a big hill. It began to buck again, so we limped into Carson City and found an auto-parts store where we could buy new filters. They allowed us to use their side parking area to change all the fuel filters, which numbered six in Asem's special system. And we decided, since it was so late, we would stay in a nearby motel for the night.

In the morning the truck behaved nicely. I had decided that if the truck was still having trouble at Lone Pine, I would have Asem drop me off there and I would hitch to the trailhead. The road to Horseshoe Meadows was narrow, steep, and curvy, with precipitous drop-offs along the outer edge. There was no place to get off the road for car trouble. But Asem trusted the truck, as it seemed to be going smoothly, even uphill. He brought me back to the place I had been two weeks before. After he left with Asemah, it felt like I had not gone home at all. Almost everything was the same—the place, the fragrance in the air, the heat. Just the people were different from those I had left.

My bear canister, which was required along the PCT through most of the Sierras, carried ten days' worth of food. It was the heaviest I had ever filled it, but I did not want to waste time going out to resupply. I planned to hike all the way to Red's Meadow, where I could get on a bus to Mammoth Lakes for a good rest. I hoped there was enough food to give me the energy I needed. I knew of exit trails along the way, and of other resorts where food could be obtained in an emergency. But I hoped it was enough.

I lay in my tent in the campground listening to others as they sang and laughed around their campfires. Earplugs helped to muffle the late night party hubbub, and sleep came at last.

As usual in the mountains, I woke with the birds…and I was ready to continue my walk through grief on the PCT.

CHAPTER 15

Back on the Trail

It was early morning when I left Horseshoe Meadows. Light was just beginning to brighten the eastern sky. I tiptoed past big tents filled with sleeping campers whose cars were lined up in the nearby parking lot. At the western edge of the campground, I crunched past the restroom building on light-gray grit on my way toward Cottonwood Pass and the PCT. The center of the wide trail had been churned and softened by packhorses, so I stepped on the firmer edges.

While the trail followed a path through woods at the side of a huge, open field of green, hills circled the meadow, and the rising sun lit their tops with ever-growing caps of gold. Birds chirped merrily through the branches of the sparse trees that parted every so often to grant a view of the surrounding mountains. Several trails descended from the PCT to the meadow, each one from a different dip between hills. The trail to Cottonwood Pass was the steepest, near its top end, but it was also the farthest north on the ridge, and that is why I had chosen it as an exit trail. After a long, flat approach, I climbed the rocky switchbacks I had come down two weeks prior and finally topped out at a viewpoint overlooking Horseshoe Meadows.

Would I find anyone I knew up there?

I doubted it. They would be two weeks ahead.

The full bear canister and the heavier sleeping gear strained the muscles of my shoulders and back, and taxed my heart. My hope was that as I ate the food each day, the burden on both my heart and back would grow less and less. Even with the steep access trail behind me, I had to stop often to rest.

I expected to meet only new people, but the first person joyously greeting me was "Tumbleweed," whom I had met near Big Bear City. She was nearly seventy years old and chose to keep her mileage low, so she had gotten behind. After the cheerful reunion, I left her sitting on a rock at the edge of the trail, calling out good wishes to me as I turned to the north.

At dusk I reached Crabtree Meadows, where a side trail led to Mt. Whitney, the tallest peak in the contiguous forty-eight states. I had already climbed Mt. Whitney in the past, so I meant to forego that adventure this time. At Crabtree Meadows several small tents lay within scattered notches among the trees at the edge of softly winding Whitney Creek. I chose a flat spot and bantered with the other thru-hikers camped there. I tried and failed to ignore my toes, but they hurt more than my shoulders for some reason. *Could it be the new hiking shoes? Or was it just that I had been off the trail for two weeks, and my feet had lost their trail hardening?* There didn't seem to be enough room in the toe box. I removed the insoles to inspect the volume within each box and found the culprits. I had left the original insoles inside the shoes and added my custom ones on top. Taking out the factory ones brought back the roomy comfort I had expected from the new shoes.

Morning brought more blue sky, and lots of old memories. One of my favorite places along the PCT was the Bighorn Plateau, and I savored it as I climbed the trail to pass a tarn that mirrored a few puffy clouds in the deep blue sky. Tyndall Creek, less than knee deep, proved easy to cross this time. And memories of past hikes, when I could call Adnan and exclaim over the scenery, bubbled into my consciousness as I pushed through the low-lying, frothy water. Forester Pass was up ahead—a challenge for the next day. *Would there be snow to cross or thunderstorms to dodge?* I put those thoughts out of my mind for the evening and sat by the creek to allow my feet the luxury of dangling in ice-cold water, while the sun dipped behind the trees at my back and the hilltops to the east turned brilliant gold with alpenglow.

Solo in the High Sierra

CHAPTER 16

Forester Pass

MY HEART GALLOPING IN MY chest, I climbed the final rocky steps to the top of Forester Pass, the highest pass on the PCT at 13,153 feet of elevation. I was alone…I had been for hours. Letting my heart slow down, I removed my pack and sat on one of the jutting rocks at the crest. Wind blew across the gap, but it was not cold enough to hide from it. Wind felt good on my sweat-soaked face, reddened from exposure to the elements and from the exertion of the climb.

Trail on the south side of Forester Pass

I looked at the sign marking the narrow pass on the steep and jagged ridge. The last time I stood there by the sign, I remembered, I had talked with my sweet husband Adnan by cell phone. It was the previous year on a hike of the John Muir Trail (JMT) with my friend Ann, and Adnan had alarmed me with news that he did not feel well.

"You will be shocked at how much weight I have lost," he had said when we talked by phone during my breakfast at the motel in Independence earlier that morning. I almost aborted that trip to go home in case his illness was something awful—a word I could not speak, but that screamed loudly in my head—*cancer*. He told me he was sure that it was just the change in his diabetes medicine that was making him feel unwell.

"Stay on your hike, Ya Albe," he had said. "Call me when you can, but I am sure I am really okay."

I was hesitant about heading back out to the access trail over Kearsarge Pass and on to the JMT. I was glad only a week or so remained until I could return home and delve into the matter of his health to get to the bottom of the issues that kept him feeling ill.

That summer of 2013, I stood at this very spot and found cell service, elated to be able to hear his voice again, especially since it was reassuring.

"Do you hear (*huff, huff*) how well I feel (*huff, puff*) this morning?" he had asked, sounding out-of-breath but cheerful. "Can you tell? I am (*huff, huff*) on the treadmill!"

That conversation had allowed my fears to subside. *He must be okay! He is on the treadmill!* I had thought. And Ann and I descended south from Forester Pass through approaching thunderclouds that could not quell my lifted spirits. *He was okay!*

But he was not okay. If I called him now, he could not answer. He had died from pancreatic cancer a few months after I had made that phone call from this spot. Oh yes. I really *was* alone.

I could still call my son Asem, though. I could let him know I had made it this far and reassure myself that he and my little granddaughter Asemah had made it safely down the road from Horseshoe Meadows, where they had dropped me off, and that they had arrived at their home in Phoenix. I took the cell phone off airplane mode. There was no service. I climbed a few of the boulders to a higher position to see if service would be available in a better location. Still there was no cell service. *How had I been able to call my husband from here the previous year?* I had been lucky back then! I had needed Adnan's voice to quiet the misgivings I had had about staying on the trail. This year, Asem's voice would have helped me to relax about his possibly ailing truck, but he was healthy, strong, smart…and a good driver. These thoughts heartened my spirits, and I turned my attention outward once again.

To the south I could see the trail and the distant hills through which I had traveled during the day. The trail looked like a long, undulating ribbon from here, until it disappeared into the trees on the far horizon, deep in the valley that was surrounded by rocky peaks. I had passed through one of my favorite parts of the trail this morning. I loved the tarn and the rolling hills through the Bighorn Plateau.

Once, the first time I had passed through the plateau, my back had been hurting so badly that I could not enjoy the area fully. That was back in 2008, during my first thru-hike attempt of the PCT. I was last in line of our little group of thru-hikers; our trail names were "Tailwinds," "Tahoe Mike," "Southern Man," "Vegematic," and (me) "Blue Butterfly." We had made a pact to cross the Sierras together for safety. "One Step," a dear friend from home, had also been in the pact with us, but she had left the trail at Lone Pine to rest and later had been airlifted by helicopter from Purple Lake, near Silver Pass, because a bleeding stomach ulcer had bled her energy away to almost nothing.

As our little group struggled through the cold wind that scoured the Bighorn Plateau that year, exhaustion, hunger, and back pain drained my reserves. I allowed my mind to create a pleasant space where it could wander and daydream to help me cope with the discomfort. In that mind place, I had a plate of food with savory baked chicken, browned and moist. Beside the chicken were mashed potatoes, dripping with butter, and steamed green beans (also with butter), and a side plate of hot apple pie permeated with cinnamon. My daydream seemed so real that I could actually smell it! My mouth watered at the thought.

In my mind, after sitting in a cushioned easy chair to eat the deliciousness, I let my dream move to a hot, cleansing shower, and afterward, Adnan helped me into a warm, fluffy robe, bright red in color. He hugged me in my imagining, swaying back and forth as if rocking me for comfort. I actually felt myself being lifted to a soft bed, and I heard his deep voice quietly saying sweet words that brought serenity. This imagined world of peace and comfort was suddenly shattered.

"There's Tyndall Creek!" Tahoe Mike shouted back to the group, his muffled voice cutting in and out because of the gusty wind.

His words had smashed my daydreams and made them float away like smoke. Pain reared back up into my consciousness. Reality was back, and energy drained away as I followed the group to the edge of the tumultuous water as it raged and surged its way past the crossing point. It roared and frothed, smothering our shouting voices as we tried to communicate and safely cross.

Southern Man helped me to ford the river, as I was unsteady and feared that I might slip and fall into the cold, unfriendly waters. The sun had dipped below the ridges in the west, and darkness was upon us. When I shakily reached the far side, I found a spot among the trees to set up my camp. A little piece of closed-cell foam, which I used as a sit pad, was missing. It must have been blown off my pack by one of the severe wind gusts up on the plateau, or maybe I had lost it during the creek crossing.

The pain I had been feeling in my lower back that day turned out to be a hike-ender. When I had descended with the group through Kearsarge Pass to resupply in the town of Independence, the pain had increased to the point that I had to go home. I thought after a rest I could come back to finish my thru-hike. I did not know at the time that my lower back was honeycombed with multiple stress fractures. I was not allowed to return to the trail for the rest of the summer.

This morning, on my grief walk of the PCT, I had hiked over the Bighorn Plateau in bright sunlight and pleasant temperatures. My healed back had given me no trouble, and my energy levels had been high. The sweet little tarn sparkled, yet reflected the bare rolling hill behind it. The clear air smelled of flowers and alpine grasses. As I rock-hopped across Tyndall Creek, which gently swirled its way along instead of raging this year, my eyes had searched the horizon for the crack in the far rocky ridge that was Forester Pass.

Here I was, now, on top. I turned to the north. The descent could be tricky. Several feet of soft snow covered much of the trail near the top, except for the first few feet along the ridge. Holes told me that others had punched through the snow with their steps, "postholing" as it is called. I could see smaller patches of snow on the less steep parts of the upper reaches of the valley, but I could not see the trail farther on. I knew it followed Bubbs Creek through the trees that choked the groove in the deep valley spread out into the distance.

Shouldering my pack, I started down. My mind had been wandering again—remembering past times along this part of the trail. It was time to come back to reality. Alone, I needed to get down to safer ground and camp somewhere along the creek.

Looking at Forester Pass from the north, amid snow patches and talus rock

The trail disappeared in the snowbank about twenty feet along the ridge. Carefully, I stepped onto the soft, dirty white slush.

Schwoosh, clunk. My foot sank to the rock below.

Firm snow along the ridges of the pockmarks created by sun and wind (sun cups, as they are called) helped me along the way, but soft patches formed a network of danger. If a leg punched through and my body kept going, I could break the leg or hyperextend a knee. Uneven chunks of rock slept below the snowfield. The relatively flat trail zigzagged underneath, but its course could not be seen, except in a few places where the snow had melted farther down. I used my trekking poles to test the strength of each spot my feet intended to use. Sometimes I had to skirt the edge of an area that promised post-holing, stepping on wet or icy rock surfaces, none of them level, using a trekking pole on a downhill rock to brace against.

I looked back up at Forester Pass. It was deserted. Slowly and gingerly I made my way down to a bit of visible trail and nearly fell onto a rock with relief. My leg muscles cramped from the struggle.

"Oh God! This is dangerous! Help me!" I pleaded silently. "Help me make it safely down!"

Each section of trail I completed generated a bit more relief. The pass was getting farther away, and the stunted trees of the upper valley looked closer. I could not really rest until my feet stood on bare trail at the bottom of the steepest part, past the gray, rocky stacks and ridges, past the churning waterfalls from the melting snow, past the place where growing things struggled for a foothold.

With the light fading, I continued with less strain through pristine meadows, past smaller waterfalls, and over boggy parts of the trail where the snow had recently melted. The air smelled of pine and mud. Shoots of new little plants poked through the smoothed surface of the ground. Relief of having gotten past the disintegrating snow slope welled within, and I began a quicker descent to look for a camp.

Darkness was near when I smelled the smoke of a campfire. Laughter curled out from a spot below in the trees, and my feet were drawn toward the sound.

They were sitting around a dancing fire, tents surrounding the exuberant group of young people. A small flat area in between fallen logs, big enough for my tent, invited me in.

"Could I join you in your campsite tonight?" I inquired hopefully.

"Sure!" replied a gleeful voice. "After you set up, you could join us for a game of 'mafia'!"

I didn't know the game of "mafia," but I was more than willing to try it. I stumbled in and dropped my pack with a thud. Exhaustion compelled me to set up the tent and just sleep, but loneliness had been creeping into my countenance. I yearned for the company of others, especially others who laughed and whose jovial voices rang out to support and hold my soul steady.

Three of the campfire participants were young male hikers going south on the John Muir Trail. Three others were young female PCT thru-hikers who had come over the pass earlier than I. They were already down in the trees when I had stood on top of Forester Pass, alone. I shared a log by the fire, listening to their laughter. Camaraderie cemented these hikers who had been thrown together, all passionate about the trail but not having known each other in regular life. I realized that we were all sisters and brothers there around that fire. The fact that I was much older than the others, and a grandmother, did not matter. I was a trail person. That was all that counted.

I crawled into my warm sleeping bag that night content, with tendrils of camaraderie still enveloping my spirit. I had hiked twenty miles that day over Forester Pass—a long way for a hiker of any age in the High Sierras—but I still had a long way to go before I could get off and rest in a real bed. For now my fluffy bag felt wonderful. The warm bed from my daydreams of the past, with the memory of Adnan whispering sweetness into my ears, drifted back into my real dreams, to comfort me during a deep and restful sleep.

CHAPTER 17

Glen and Pinchot

IN THE CHILLY MORNING, I stepped out of the tent to look at the campfire ring, no longer alive with dancing flames circled by laughing hikers. None had yet awoken from sleep except me, an early riser. The camaraderie of the evening and a good rest had bolstered my spirits, and I set out northward on descending trail. Pebbles and mud bogs filled the narrow path, and small forest plants bent over the trail edges, heavily laden with dew. I crunched my way down to the base of a steep, zigzagging ascent to a junction with an exit trail over Kearsarge Pass to the town of Independence. I did not want to take that trail for resupplying, as I hoped to catch up with some of the friends who had been with me before Father's Day.

Before climbing, I turned my face back toward Vidette, my favorite mountain of the High Sierras, with its lofty peak piercing a blue morning sky. How magnificent it was!

With determination, I began to climb.

The skimpy food left in my bear canister worried me. At the upper junction with the exit trail, I sat on a downed log and opened the food canister to count the items inside and consider if I should go out or not. The rocky ridge of Glen Pass perched a short distance from my rest spot, and lovely Rae Lakes, with alpine trees and charming meadows, awaited. I chose to risk it, despite the meager rations.

Over Glen Pass, down past Rae Lakes, I moved toward the deep forest of Woods Creek where I camped for the night.

Mount Vidette

Brrrrr! It was cold there!

As I snuggled into fluffy warmth, I was glad I had bought a better sleeping bag when I left the trail for the Father's Day interlude.

The next day I hiked up and over Pinchot Pass, the trail winding through monolithic boulders. Southbound hikers had warned me that the pass was a difficult part of the trail, but I found it manageable, probably because I crossed it in the early part of the day.

Thoughts of Adnan came and went as I wandered up and down, past meadows and lakes, with gray, craggy peaks keeping watch in the near distance. *How I longed to tell him of the beauty!*

Late in the afternoon, I came to the South Fork King River, which crashed through a tree-laden landscape. It split in places, and I tried to search for the easiest crossing on logs, as I could see no bridge. A web of makeshift trails told me others had needed to do the same. One of the divergent streams had no log, but a few submerged rocks poked their tops above the shallow, swirling water. It seemed harmless to me, as it was not one of the deep rivulets. I tried to rock-hop it, but the span between the little islands of rock was too far.

Splash!

My left foot plunged into the water, soaking the shoe and sock, while my balance teetered and then regained itself with my trekking poles.

But this was the last of the tangle of splitting waterways to have to cross, and grateful that I had not toppled over and soaked all my clothing, I sat on a fallen log to change my socks. My left shoe still sloshed as I began to climb the long, continuous ascent to the base of Mather Pass, where I planned to spend the night.

The wind had picked up. Along the way, I stopped to talk with a couple of thru-hikers setting up a camp.

"It's going to be *cold* up there," said a woman as she shook out her sleeping bag to fluff the fill inside it. "Stay with us here!"

"I want to get closer to the pass," I said.

The amount of food in my bear canister kept me to a tight schedule, unless I decided to take time to go out to Vermilion Valley Resort or stop at the Muir Trail Ranch, and I did not want to divert from my original plan to hike all the way to Red's Meadow before I got off to resupply.

Waving, I kept going ever upward. The wind grew stronger as I climbed to an open area covered with small stones and scattered clumps of short, bushy trees. It was harsh terrain, but I knew where a few flat spots harbored within the clumps because I had stayed there when I hiked the John Muir Trail with Ann, before I lost my husband.

Nothing had changed, except that I was alone this time. I found the very spot I had used before and put my tent up on the sheltered pad, where stones had been swept away by boots in the past.

Camp just before Mather Pass

Again I listened to my sweet Adnan's voice on the MP3 player as the wind howled down from Mather Pass across the landscape, while I huddled within a protective cocoon of nylon and down feathers.

CHAPTER 18

The Epiphany

AT THE BASE OF MATHER Pass, I awoke in my tent to wind and a threatening sky. *Brrr!* The cold wormed its way through my sleeping clothes and settled around my core. I hoped I would warm up with movement, and after packing up, I started toward the pass. But as the wind increased, my nylon hiking pants could not stop the penetrating chill. I had to stop in the partial shelter of a large boulder to stretch into more protective clothing.

Somewhat relieved with a bit of warmth, I pushed on, but the dark clouds soon began to pelt me with small droplets of sideways flying rain. Just as I stopped to unpack the rain poncho, a man approached from Mather. He had crossed over the pass as the storm moved in, and he helped me to get the poncho over the top of my pack so I could zip the sides. Too cold for chitchat, I thanked him and he headed south with a smile and a quick wave of his hand.

As I hiked up the switchbacks toward the top of the pass, the rain turned to sleet—and at the top, heavy wind blew hard snow pellets that stung my face. On the north side, though, the wind decreased and the showers diminished and finally stopped. The sun peeked out between clouds to dry my gear as I lunched near the top of the Golden Staircase, a steep rocky path with short zigzags that descended into the next valley.

In that valley was an exit trail called Bishop Pass. Near the junction I noticed a deer sniffing at a cook pot near a tent. The hiker in the campsite had his back turned, so I called to him to warn him of the lurking deer. The man was eighty years old and told me he was a failure, because he had only hiked half of the JMT and needed to bail.

"You are an inspiration to me," I said. "I hope I can still hike when I am eighty!"

Waving, I moved on toward my next camp, a meadow before the climb to Muir Pass. Adnan wandered in and out of my dreams that night. I awoke with a sense of excitement, knowing that Muir Pass is incredibly beautiful and I would walk there this day, once again. As I packed up, the dreams of Adnan flickered around my thoughts, comforting me, reminding me that he was, and would always be, a big part of my life.

Clear and fresh, the morning air energized me as I ascended toward the pass. The trail traversed rocky stretches and followed switchbacks as it steepened, with gleaming ponds spotting the lower reaches, and little cascading streams connecting them, the water flowing from the upper ponds down into the lower parts of the valley, making a pearly chain of lakes.

The higher I climbed, the more I had to struggle with the effort. Rocks crunched under my feet, my breath coming in heaving gasps. The pointed, round roof of the Muir Hut stood above the boulder fields, identifiable only by shape, as the color was gray like the rest of the landscape. A woman waved to me from the door and welcomed me as I got closer and could see her face.

"Come inside and get out of the wind," she said.

I dropped my pack and followed her into the dark, musty circular room. Several hikers occupied the continuous bench that lined the inside edges except for a small section that displayed a plaque explaining the history of the hut. The stone shelter was built in 1930 through the generous donation of G. F. Schwarz, a member of the Sierra Club, and it was dedicated to John Muir.

I had not seen anyone for hours, so I responded to the warm, happy greetings with a big smile that crinkled my eyes. "Half Double" and his wife, "Shiney," I had not seen since Hauser Creek at the beginning of the trail. "Any Minute Now," the woman who had invited me in, was new to me, but we chattered together as if we had been friends for years.

Muir Hut

The river crossing of Evolution Creek was ahead of us, farther down the enchanting valley. The ford has struck fear into the hearts of many a hiker over the years. The lazy river moved slowly, but its depth spawned the stories of hikers losing traction and being swept downstream. Any Minute Now worried about the ford.

"Would you camp with me on this side of the river and cross with me in the morning?" she asked.

We camped in the woods and waited for dawn to arrive, when rivers are usually shallower because of the cooler night temperatures slowing the melting of snow. But Evolution Creek was only knee deep this time. Laughing with relief on the other side, Any Minute Now took a moment to smoke her pipe as her eyes scanned the river. I had crossed the flowing water with flip flops that were tied to my ankles by a pair of bright blue shoelaces, and I used our rest time to change back into my shoes. We hiked together the rest of the day and camped at Sallie Keyes Lake.

That evening, I watched Any Minute Now cast her fishing line out into the lake, over and over, her pipe hanging from her lips. Mosquitoes hovered around our warm bodies and above the still water of the lake, but repellent kept them from biting us. Trout were jumping, creating little rippled circles on the surface of the lake, and each cast of the line filled me with hope for her to catch a fish.

The line went taut, the end of the pole bent down with strain, and Any Minute Now tensed with excitement.

"I've got one!" she said.

I watched with fascination as she reeled in the line and brought a beautiful trout of some variety to the bank.

She shared her fish with me that night, cooking on a gravelly spot near the lake, far from our tents so that no food odors would interest any wandering animals during the night.

Any Minute Now fishing in Sallie Keyes Lake

We tried to hike together the next day as well, but Any Minute Now struggled to keep up with me, and she decided to slow down to keep her strength. Both of us had resupply boxes waiting at the Motel 6 in Mammoth Lakes.

"I hope to see you in Mammoth!" I said as I waved and continued down the trail. She was smoking her pipe, sitting on a log, her face red from exertion. Her genuine smile lifted my spirits, but I had to keep going. I could not slow down, or I might run out of food before I could get out of the mountains.

At the bottom of a long descent I found the side trail to Vermilion Valley Resort. *Should I go out? No. That would add a couple of days to my hike through the High Sierras, and I didn't want that.*

I did not tarry. I wanted to reach a camping area that was just a couple of miles south of Silver Pass. Since my chosen destination was nearly twenty miles from Sallie Keyes Lake, it would require extraordinary effort to make it that far by nightfall. A steep rocky climb stood between my goal and me. Though my shoulders burned from the long day of carrying a pack, my rest breaks had to be short in order to have enough time.

The trail approached a massive cliff face. I looked where the map said the trail ascended, and I could see a few steps, but it seemed to go straight up! The first group of steps took me to a short level walkway, only to present another stairway of rock. Some of the steps were too big for my legs, and I grunted with effort while my knees and thighs screamed. After what seemed like hours, I began to hope I might reach the top where the trail eased to a gradual incline. But it just kept going, and frustration took over. *Would it never end? Would I be climbing rocky steps forever? Was I in some kind of purgatory where I would climb throughout eternity?*

By the time I reached the point above the cliff where the trail moderated, the sun had dropped low in the sky. The sight of the deserted camp brought relief as I stumbled past a big boulder and dropped my pack in the dirt.

It was at Silver Pass the next morning that I had an epiphany. Alone, I stopped to take in the beauty around me. To the south, from which I had come up the rocky trail, I could see a beautiful array of bumps and knobs. North of the pass was a deep, tree-lined valley that stretched toward the horizon. A few short alpine trees competed for space on the boulder-studded pass, and the warm morning sun lit the rocks and surrounding grit with sparkles.

The climbing part was over, and now I could rest—and enjoy!

Near Silver Pass

Enjoy? Without Adnan? Guilt crept into my heart. *I am supposed to be in mourning!*

My washing-machine mind continued to churn. When my kids were little, I remembered my husband saying to them, "Put yourself in the other person's shoes. That way, you will know how they are thinking."

Well, how about this? Let me put myself in your *shoes, sweetie! What if I was the one who had died? How would I want* you *to live?*

The epiphany hit me. I would want Adnan to live with joy! I would want him to laugh, to savor the life left to him!

Duh! That's how he wants me to live!

It's okay to laugh with friends and to enjoy the beauty through which I walk. I will remember Adnan forever, but I must allow myself to live with the happiness he has always wished for me.

Contentment replaced the guilt that had encroached upon my heart. My steps felt lighter as I descended from Silver Pass.

Happiness is good! And it will honor Adnan to allow it!

Yes. Oh yes.

CHAPTER 19

A Flood of Words

I REACHED RED'S MEADOW AND the bus to Mammoth Lakes at breakfast time. Oh, how hungry I was! It had been nine and a half days since I had been dropped off at Horseshoe Meadows, and my bear canister was nearly empty. "Switcheroo" had given me a couple of bars to help fill my nutritional needs, and a JMT hiker had unloaded his peanut M&M's into my stash, but the food I had carried was long gone and my clothes seemed much too large. I had to cinch my pants up with a cord in the belt loops to keep them from falling off. The shirt that had fit when I bought it was now so large that I could hardly see my form within it.

I ate a plate of eggs and hash browns at the restaurant at Red's Meadow and followed it with an ice-cream bar before the bus ride. In Mammoth Lakes I had a burger and milkshake after checking in at the Motel 6. I was still hungry.

Throughout the town, thru-hikers lounged in motels, restaurants, and at Schat's Bakery, where I bought a bag of goodies to assuage my flaming hunger. Any Minute Now checked into the Motel 6 later that day, but she decided she needed more rest than one night, so we would not be hiking together after all. I probably should have stayed another night as well, to bolster the food intake for more energy, but I was anxious to continue on the trail. I visited Any Minute Now in the morning but then was on my way to catch a bus back to the Mammoth Ski Area, where I could transfer to the Red's Meadow Shuttle.

Back on the trail, I took a few minutes to enjoy fleeting views of the Devils Postpile, a national monument where giant six-sided columns of rock cluster together in exposed areas. Tourists looked like tiny dots as they snapped photos and wandered along the trail by the cliffy formations.

Alone again I climbed switchbacks up the side of a ridge and traversed it to its far end, where I camped under trees with a view of the valley below. The John Muir Trail followed the opposite wall of the valley, along a string of lakes. From my camp, I could see the shimmering of one of the pristine lakes, but I did not know which one it was.

The next morning, still alone, I followed the trail down to the bottom of the valley and arrived early in the day at Thousand Island Lake.

Thousand Island Lake

I could see where it got its name! Poking out of the water were countless islands of rock. Behind the lake rose the monoliths of Mt. Ritter and Banner Peak.

I sat on a rock at the lake's edge, watching water bugs skittering on the surface. The beauty around me seemed like a blanket, and I relaxed into it, opening my mind to whatever would come. A dam within me seemed to break apart, and words spilled over the edge and demanded to be written down. I had a small baggie with a pen and a few folded pages of school notebook paper, and the words began to rush out of me. I could not stop the flow. Nor could I stop the tears from dropping onto the pages with the words.

In the back of my rational mind, I realized that people had congregated behind my lakeside rock, but I could no more stop the words than to stop a waterfall until I had come to the end of the first batch telling of the wrenching of my sweetheart out of my life. I took a deep breath, looking out over the lake, and I knew without a doubt, there would be more stories to tell.

The people behind me had moved on, except for their leader. It turned out that they were a trail-work crew, and the leader was waiting for a few stragglers. I apologized for ignoring him and his group, but seeing my tear-streaked face, he listened as I explained my reason for being on the trail, the story of my grief.

"Can I hug you?" he asked.

I just reached for him and felt the comfort of a stranger, another human being on the same path as all of us are, who will some day leave this earth like Adnan did, from one cause or another.

A short time later, I reached Island Pass, where several small lakes fill the dips between rock-studded plains, with scattered tree clumps near the waterways. When I stopped to rest, more words pressed forward to tumble out onto the rest of the notebook paper, until all the lines were filled and I had to write in the margins. Three hours later I realized that time was getting away from me, and I wanted to be on the other side of Donahue Pass before dark. My mind raced, and events of the grief walk jostled around in the soup of my thoughts, arranging themselves into an order that could be remembered by phrases, which I listed in a blank part of one of the margins on a random page.

By the time I reached Tuolumne Meadows, the words had settled some but still agitated against the gate of my mind, waiting for more paper, which nestled with the food and supplies in a box at the Tuolumne Meadows Post Office.

That night I camped with other thru-hikers in the backpacker campsite in the very center of the Tuolumne Meadows General Campground. Vehicles, music, bicycles, RVs, campfires—these were front-country camp styles that seemed foreign to me, so different from the lifestyle I had been living. Still, at the backpacker campsite, a spread of small tents surrounded the picnic tables, campfire rings, and bear boxes, a little bit apart from the car camping area. The store with all its treats, a fast food café, a real bathroom with "flushy" toilets, and garbage and recycle bins gave us a feeling of living in luxury.

At the store every outlet was used for charging phones, and every bench was occupied by tourists or by hikers going through resupply boxes or waiting for shuttles. Happy talk bubbled around the various groups sharing experiences of the trail or of whatever adventures the participants were on.

As darkness fell I got out my precious stash of new paper and began to add to my story.

"Tink" squatted down beside me.

"What are you writing?" she asked.

I told her about my growing desire to share my grief walk with family and friends, and maybe even publish it for others, so that someone else who might be grieving could possibly find comfort and direction through my writing.

"Is it just for widows?"

"I don't know," I said. "Maybe it could help with other kinds of grief…"

And then she told me her own story. Little Tink, delicate and tiny like her namesake fairy, had suffered an experience with the death of her boyfriend six years earlier. He had committed suicide, and Tink was still in the depths of grief over it. Her own mother had died just a month or so before we met at Tuolumne Meadows, but she expressed little feeling about the recent event.

"My mother was not a mother to me," she said. "She was a drug addict, and my sister and I raised ourselves."

When she spoke of the boyfriend, tears streamed down her cheeks and her voice broke.

"I feel unworthy," she said. "I never had a mother, and the man I loved killed himself. I think maybe I don't deserve to be loved."

I thought about her story and my heart went out to her. At least I had a great love, and I am thankful for the years I had with him. How I wished I could find an answer for her, this woman who had only felt love from a boyfriend who checked out of life.

Later, I thought, the fact that she expressed anger that she was not raised by a loving mother tells me that she does feel worthy inside. If she was not angry about it, she would accept being unworthy. But anger says she feels she deserves love! (I never got to tell her these thoughts, though, because they did not bubble up in my washing-machine mind until the next day on the trail.)

Before I could sleep that night, I listened to a story of a different kind of grief.

A woman who had owned a guiding business lost it over ethics. The company that shunted clients her way wanted her to take anyone who applied. Sometimes she refused a client who was so out-of-shape that it would have been unsafe, in her opinion, to take the person on the kind of arduous hikes she led into remote places. So the company began to shunt the clients elsewhere, and her business withered to the point of collapse. She grieved the loss of the business that years of her life had been devoted to building.

So many kinds of grief hit people in different ways. How can my story help people who suffer other kinds of losses? As each person is individual, each loss comes with its own pain. My only hope is that maybe some small thing in my experience will tip a sorrowful person toward a healing path.

I slept that night with gratitude. In my case I deeply grieved, because I had been deeply loved! This journey had shown me a way to begin to cope with my great loss, though I knew it was just a fledgling start to the process.

There would be more teachings from the trail…oh yes…there would be more!

Frayed Edges

CHAPTER 20

Moving on from Tuolumne

I DESCENDED THE PACKED DIRT trail from the backpacker campsite, a cool breeze chilling my face in the early morning. The cloudless sky promised warmth, but for now, I needed my puffy jacket. It had been too early to say good-bye to my new friends, as they showed no signs of activity within their shelters. So alone I trudged on, stopping first at the big green garbage bin behind the store. Campfire smoke still drifted among the car camps, but no people moved about.

I crossed a deserted highway to walk the trail north toward Glen Aulin, one of the Sierra high camps that was staffed during the summer months. Somewhere within the first hour I passed a hollow tree, reminding me of the vacant place in my heart, and I thought about the previous evening…how interacting with others had kept the loneliness at bay. The numbness was gradually beginning to wear off. Now, alone, the pain of separation from my beloved came in waves. When I could meet and talk with others, though, it receded a bit. Then I could laugh, listen, and feel alive.

I realized that interaction with others would be the key for me to find joy. Even if I went to Disneyland alone to watch others relishing group fun, I would still feel isolated. In order to fill the void in my heart, I would need to seek and maintain friendships with others.

The trail took me past a wide, postcard-worthy waterfall, Tuolumne Falls, and soon I found myself among the white tents of Glen Aulin. I had not had any coffee that morning, so I sought out the store, hoping to find some. The sign on the door said "Closed." Disappointed I began to move on toward the riverside for a rest.

"Can I help you?" said a cheerful male voice from within the store as the door squeaked open.

"I was hoping for coffee," I said. "But I think you're closed."

"I think I could find you some!"

Leaving my pack outside on the step, I entered a small room with a couple of tables and a counter. I heard clanking and rummaging behind a backroom door. The bearded young man returned with a steaming cup of bitter coffee.

"I'm sorry, it's kind of old. This was from breakfast, and it's the bottom of the pot."

"Thank you!" I said. And I took it with both hands, feeling appreciative.

"Do you need anything else from the store?" he asked.

"I thought it was closed," I said.

"Well, I could open it just for you!" he said.

His friendly attitude pushed back the morose feelings that had gripped my morning walk.

"I would love to have some of those," I said, pointing to a yellow package of peanut M&M's.

My spirits rejuvenated by coffee and chocolate, I headed north on the trail once more. Along the way I spotted "Apache," "Doc," and "Red Baron" perched on a rocky cliff just above the trail, having a break. I stopped to banter with them a bit, calling them "slackers" for their frequent rests. Laughing, they sent me on with a cheerful "See you soon!" Of course, they would. They were young and fast, no matter how rugged the terrain.

And the terrain became rugged indeed, with steep ups and downs. Rocks and big steps riddled the way, and my chest heaved with effort to keep going. I had to stop more frequently to let my heart rate slow on the uphill parts. I wondered if I was eating enough. The struggle seemed to be more intense the farther north I went.

I crossed a stream and the trail eased through a forest, with evening approaching. Searching for a campsite, I found one behind a downed log with plenty of room. By now clouds had moved in, and rain threatened to fall. The sky spit a few drops, then stopped, and started again sporadically.

Doc passed my campsite and chose another spot nearby. When I greeted him, he seemed reticent, so I left him with his solitude and went to the stream for water.

With morning came blue skies again. The tent would need to be dried in the sun, if possible. I really hated to carry a wet tent.

The terrain had not changed. Though camp had been in a small flat forest, the steep hills took over again. I found Doc sitting by a rock in the sun, so I stopped to join him as our gear dried spread over branches and other rocks, and we had lunch together.

"I don't know if I want to stay out here on the trail," he said. "I've been having a hard time."

"I know what you mean," I said. "It's tough here! I didn't remember this part being so hard! Why did you decide to thru-hike?"

"It's been a dream I've had for a long time. How 'bout you?" he asked.

"I hiked the PCT in sections, but now I am here to walk through grief. I lost my husband to cancer in March. But you know? I'm so grateful for having had him in my life for forty-eight years. And I'm grateful for having the health and the chance to be out here, right now, on the PCT."

Doc looked at me. Through a mouthful of crackers, he said, "Thank you." That was all.

Doc having lunch among some rocks, protected from bugs by a head net

It seemed that gratitude was medicine for both of us. Our spirits lifted, and we laughed as I tried to cross a river on rocks and slipped to my knees in the water at the far edge, trying to step up onto the bank. Oh well! My shoes would dry out walking. Doc's cheerful good-bye wave told me his resolve to stay on the trail had been bolstered.

Beauty in the rugged terrain

My own resolve was still in question, though. My attitude had improved, but my body seemed exhausted. The climb to Sonora Pass drained my energy reserves, though the area was beautiful with its *Sound of Music* hills and breathtaking views. My spirits sagged as I hiked along talus slopes through a narrow, cliffy notch.

I reached the road with little energy left. The signs of towns in either direction invited me to ease and comfort...to give up...to end the walk.

Should I do it? Should I just go home? I could hitch to Bridgeport. The bus to Reno goes through there...

Reason, with what was left of my resolve, prompted me to cross the road to a picnic table to eat something and rest before making a decision. As I sat there, though, I watched a hiker move to a spot to hitch in the direction of Bridgeport.

And my hands grabbed my gear and both feet moved without hesitation toward the hiker—to join him in full retreat.

At Bridgeport I signed into a motel and afterward called Tameem.

"I am coming home," I said. "I'm just too exhausted to continue."

"Now, Mama!" he said. "You told me you would not quit on a bad day, or when you were tired. Sleep on it. See if you still feel that way in the morning. And call me!"

Of course, my resolve to continue returned with a good rest and some real food—plenty of good calories marched around within my system, sprucing up the muscles and cells with enough energy to take away my sagging spirits. And I found myself by the road with my thumb out, the backpack at my feet.

"You look like one of my tribe!" said a man in a blue sedan. "Can I get you to the trail?"

Smiling, I tossed my pack in the back seat and accepted his offer. He was a climber of major mountains, and our various adventures fueled an animated conversation all the way to the trailhead.

I stepped out of the car onto blacktop and saw the picnic table where I had almost given up. With new energy I turned upward to follow a trail through an open, dry meadow, dotted with little circles of trees. Something did not seem right about it, though. I opened Halfmile's app to see that the PCT had actually started west of the parking lot, and this was a different trail! Following the directions given by the app, I was able to walk cross-country to meet the PCT as it ascended some hills to the north. This little side adventure was not to be the only exciting part of the next few days.

CHAPTER 21

A Fearless Attitude

BREATHING IN TIME WITH MY upward steps and my poles that clanked against chunks of granite, I reached the crest of the hill. The distant drone from cars on the road to Bridgeport began to recede as I started down the backside and chose a rocky perch to rest. Clouds framed the sky along the edges, but the sun shone down as I took off my shoes and socks to let my toes breathe. I found a packet of M&M's in my food bag, now free from the bear canister, which I had mailed home from Bridgeport.

As I munched and watched the puffy clouds move around the sky, a young bearded man approached and dropped his pack to sit across from me for his own rest. Joined by a couple more of his friends, they all decided lunchtime had arrived, and soon, animated conversation flew back and forth across the trail along with the sharing of cheese and crackers, nuts, and candy bars.

I watched as one of the hikers took an empty, plastic water bottle from his pack. It had a strange looking attachment to the side. Laughter erupted from the group.

"Want some weed?" asked one of them as he stretched the homemade water pipe toward me with a big smile that showed through his light-brown beard.

Surprised that anyone would ask me that, I laughed and said, "No, thanks! I don't do that stuff."

"Okay," he said, and he began a smoking ritual to share among the others.

I excused myself as soon as I thought polite and continued on the trail that contoured the ridges toward the north. The clouds had puffed themselves into a boiling mass with a promise of thunder, and I wanted to top the next ridge before strikes of lightning could be a problem. But I could not make it. I had to stop early and cover my gear until the afternoon storm fell apart.

When it felt safe, I topped the ridge. My rain gear was wet, but the rest of my things had been protected.

Early evening found me at the base of a low, wooded hill. A flat spot near its crown appealed to me for a camp. Though no water source flowed near it, I did not need any extra water. I had filled my containers at the last stream and had enough for the night. I kicked a couple of fallen branches out of the way and set up my tent.

"Nice camp!" said "Testament," the apparent leader of the weed-smoking group as they kept pace with each other.

"Thanks!" I said. "There's plenty of room here."

"We need to get to the next water source," said Testament cheerfully.

They disappeared down the hill, and I went back to the camp chores of making dinner and preparing for the night.

Light filtered through the ceiling of the tent with the coming of dawn, waking me as it usually did. And by the time the morning light made a headlamp unnecessary, I was shuffling along the PCT where my young friends had passed the previous evening. Down a steep slope I could see their camp. All was quiet among the cluster of little tents; my silent steps would not disturb them, and I moved on.

A few minutes later, my mind churning with random thoughts, I heard a crashing noise to the left up the steep forested slope. My eyes flashed to the left and what I saw froze me to the spot. A huge, cinnamon-colored bear bounded through the trees straight toward me! His fur rippled as his powerful muscles propelled him downward, and I stood like a statue with my mouth open, with no time to even think of being scared, let alone get out a camera. When he reached a distance of about thirty feet, he looked up. His eyes registered surprise, and he flipped in midair, veering away back up the hill as fast as he could go, breaking dead branches on his way.

For a few moments, I stood without breathing, searching the place in the woods where he had disappeared from view. My tardy call of "HEY, BEAR!" was too late for the bear to even hear.

"Wow...Wow!" was all I could say.

I should have been terrified, but I was not. How lucky I felt! I felt fortunate...not that I had escaped a mauling, but that I had been allowed to see such a beautiful sight! I had met bears before, mostly in national parks, where they were used to being near people, but this one was truly wild.

I wondered if my attitude and lack of fear had to do with my desire to be with Adnan. Death did not worry me anymore. Yet I knew, somewhere deep inside, this attitude could be dangerous. My sons and grandchildren still needed me.

The euphoria of the bear encounter dissipated as the heat of the day extracted the meager energy from my system. When I reached Ebbetts Pass, new thoughts about ending the hike curled about my mind. I was still exhausted. The Bridgeport rest had not been long enough, and my energy levels slumped once again, along with my frame of mind.

Sighing, I crossed the empty highway and started up the next hill. Ahead on the trail, behind a low branch, I glimpsed a patch of blue, and I pushed the bough aside to find a plastic cooler full of fresh fruit and cookies! Oh, happy day! It was just what I needed! The trail magic provided by a generous soul sent waves of energy back into my muscles, and the thoughts of quitting the trail drained away once more.

As I walked, a herd of cows ran from me, as did a couple of deer. It seemed this old grandma was scary enough to send animals scurrying away with fear.

A peaceful night at Eagle Creek regenerated enough energy to allow me to hike twenty-three miles the next day over two big hills—The Nipple and Elephant's Back, north of which the view opened to the lovely Carson Pass. When I had hiked this part of the PCT before, I had called Adnan. Bittersweet memories swarmed my thoughts again as I passed islands of trees through vast, grassy meadows and the sun dropped low in the western sky. Darkness was descending. I would need to camp.

At Carson Pass, camping is allowed only in designated spots for which people had to preregister. But I was too late to make it all the way down to the road, where the visitor center was already closed for the night anyway.

My eyes searched in vain for a flat spot and did not find one until I reached the wilderness sign, no camping allowed there. I usually followed rules. But this time, I raced against the coming of darkness to spread my shelter beside the sign, and I camped illegally.

Would my energy come back in the morning as it had at Eagle Creek? Would I wake in time to gather my things together and arrange the makeshift campsite to look pristine before an official ranger found me? I had no idea. And I was too tired to care.

CHAPTER 22

Times of Respite

I NEED NOT HAVE WORRIED. When I woke before dawn, no one had passed my tent, and I made the site look as if I had never been there. In fact, Carson Pass itself was empty of people and cars. A weathered picnic table on a gravel patch by the road looked like a good place for a break. Soon the hiss of my stove joined the sound of the gentle breeze, and after hot coffee with a snack of dried cranberries and almonds, I packed up and crossed the road, thinking of Tammy.

South Lake Tahoe was only a few hours away by foot. Tammy, who had taken over the household chores for seven weeks during Adnan's final time with us, awaited my arrival to give me comfort, rest, love, and needed calories. When I arrived at the parking lot at Echo Lake, near the summit of Highway 50, her smile from the driver's seat of her little truck brightened my outlook, and I gratefully threw my pack and poles into the back and settled onto the cushy seat of the cab.

"Hi, Mama! I love you!" she said, reaching across to give me a one-armed hug. "We're glad you're here!"

For three days, I ate, rested, ate again, and basked in the warmth of Tammy's family and neighbors. On the second day of my stay, Corona, her yellow lab, joined us in her speedboat for a trip across the lake, where he retrieved a floating ball over and over until he collapsed on the beach. I didn't have to retrieve anything! I just rested and ate more.

The last day before I headed back to the trail, Tammy took me "rock crawling" with a few friends who had trucks with huge tires and roll bars. We slowly lurched up the steep boulder field, finally climbing to the top of a giant rock where they set up a barbecue. We watched the sun set over the western mountains through which the PCT wound its way north. Tomorrow I would walk that way, but this night, I filled my tummy with grilled steak and potato salad while relaxing and listening to animated conversation, and a growling sound from the next hill over.

"That's our local bear," Tammy said, laughing.

Rock Crawling

While lightning gave us an exciting show in the puffy clouds around the edges of the evening sky, stars began to twinkle in a donut hole of clearness above us. We quickly stowed the grill, food tubs, and trash into the trucks and bumbled our way back down the boulders. I was looking forward to one more restful night in a real bed.

Morning brought us back to Echo Lake, where I had left off. Dave, one of Tammy's neighbors, loved to hike with dogs, and he came along for the day with Corona and Shaina, another neighbor's dog, so that they could play together on the trail for a few miles. Tammy joined us for the boat ride across Echo Lake, and it was with a bit of sadness that I waved to her in the retreating boat as it bobbed on the choppy water, heading away from us.

A good-bye photo with Tammy at Echo Lake

Dave took charge of both dogs, and we entered the beautiful Desolation Wilderness that characterized the Tahoe part of the trail. White domes and slabs of weathered rock lined a string of lakes under the blue sky. Sometimes the trail consisted of a double line of stones placed on the huge slabs to indicate the trail direction. Without them, hikers could get lost, as millions of hiker footsteps did not affect the rock enough to make the path clear. The fragrance of evergreens permeated the air, and sunrays beat off the rocks, bringing warmth as well as the need for sunglasses. A light wind puffed against us as we hiked, helping to keep us from getting too hot.

The companionship was only for the day, though. Our laughter and bantering came to an end at a junction that would take Dave and the dogs down to the road that edged Lake Tahoe. And I was alone again with my washing-machine mind.

It was the next day when I saw it. Smoke curled from a stump at the top of a ridge above my camp. I had been dodging a lightning storm the previous afternoon, and I wondered if a strike had ignited the smoldering fire. I climbed the hill to investigate.

In my hands I held my drinking bottle, but it contained less than a liter of water. My gaze searched the area around the smoking stump, but I saw no one about. No streams were nearby either. The nearest water seemed to be the crashing creek at the bottom of the cliff.

I made my way through scratchy brush to the stump. No flames danced around the surface, but steam hissed loudly when I poured my insufficient water over the hottest part. *This would need to be reported!* I reached for the phone in my pocket and hit the button, but there was no cell service here.

Heading back down toward my tent, I passed a young couple, who gladly turned back to fill water containers for dumping on the stump. I also returned to the scene with more water, but between us, it still was not enough. I spent an uneasy night worrying that a forest fire could erupt at any moment.

In the morning, I climbed back to the ridge to check and found the smoke had lessened, but it still swirled in thin coils, a slight breeze sending them sideways from time to time.

It was not until I reached where the trail curved behind the ski area of Squaw Valley that I could call 911 to report the smoldering stump. I had taken a GPS reading with my phone, so I could give the exact coordinates.

In the late afternoon, as I was watching my footing on a downward section of the trail, I heard a cheerful greeting from ahead. I looked and returned the greeting, but I thought it was a couple of strangers, not expecting to meet anyone I knew.

"Don't you know me?" asked the man in the front.

I looked at him, and he looked familiar, but still, I did not recognize him from that distance. The voice sounded familiar.

"I can't believe you don't remember me!" he said with emphasis and a grin. "I'm Tahoe Mike!"

"Tahoe Mike!" I exclaimed with glee. "I never thought I'd see you here, but I should've known! You live close by, don't you?"

He introduced his hiking partner, a neighbor who was a beginning hiker.

She's lucky to have Tahoe Mike to teach her, I thought.

We sat on rocks along the trail to have a snack and a friendly visit. I let him know about the loss of Adnan. It had been six years since I had last seen him, and he had been thin and bedraggled like most long-distance hikers after several hundred miles of trail. Back then, in 2008, he had let me use his satellite phone to call Adnan when I knew I would have to leave the trail in the Sierras, when I had developed the stress fractures in my lower back. We had enjoyed several days of hiking together, along with a few others as a group.

He was still strong, and I was delighted to see him again.

Since he and his partner were hiking in the opposite direction as I was, we took leave of each other with a renewed promise to stay in touch. Alone, I headed north once more, the feeling of friendship warm in my heart.

Though my energy levels had been greatly enhanced by the restful time with Tammy, I looked forward to another rest in Truckee, where I planned to visit Louise, another of my friends, who, when I arrived, provided me with generous hospitality as well.

But those times of respite would not see me through. The trail in northern California was embedded with unanticipated obstacles.

CHAPTER 23
Tangles in the Plan

IT WAS IN SIERRA CITY, after hiking through forested mountains north of the I-80 freeway, when snags began to arise. I arrived at the only store in town at precisely 2:30 p.m., the time the post office closed. By phone I had ordered a pair of new shoes from Super Jock & Jill's in Seattle, and they had been sent through the mail several days earlier, addressed to the store, so I was not worried.

"There is only one box," said the store clerk.

"But there should be two!" I said.

"I'll look again."

She disappeared into the back of the store where piles of resupply boxes lined the shelves on one wall.

"Sorry…only one," she said regretfully.

"My shoes should be here!" I exclaimed.

"Let me go next door to the post office to see if they're there," she said.

I followed her to a window over a paint-weathered half door.

"They're here," said a harried worker from the inside.

I was relieved and ready to receive them, but she said, "I'm sorry. I can't give them to you until tomorrow."

"Why?" I asked with incredulity, my voice raised in disbelief.

"I've already signed out, and if I sign back in, I'll be in trouble with the government. You'll have to wait."

I had not planned to spend a night in Sierra City, but the trail had taught me to be flexible, so I left to look for a place to stay.

A couple of buildings down from the store I spotted a promising bed-and-breakfast-type motel.

"Sure, we have a room," said the cheerful proprietor, and I was shown to a comfortable unit.

That afternoon I stood on the front porch of the store, the only place with Internet access. I called Tameem.

"Are you home?" I asked.

"I am!" he said enthusiastically.

"Would you go into my account and help me pay my Visa bill?"

A few moments passed while he booted up his computer.

"Which one?" he said. "There are two."

"What? But I have only one!"

"There are two here," he said.

I read off the last four digits of my card number.

"That one has a balance of zero," he said.

"But it can't! I used it several times!"

I did not want to talk too freely on the front porch, as several thru-hikers perched on a bench devouring ice cream, and they were too busy eating to talk, so their ears might hear my private concerns.

"I'll call you back, sweetheart. Thanks," I said.

Confused, I wandered over to the office of the motel and asked if I could use their landline to make a call to the bank. I discovered that every Visa card that had been used at a certain restaurant in Seattle during the previous March had been compromised, and the bank had recently closed them all down and issued new cards.

"We sent you a notice in the mail," said the bank employee, as if I should have known.

"But I'm on the Pacific Crest Trail," I said. "I have been gone almost three months."

"We sent you a new card," said the employee, not seeming to understand my words.

"It's probably in a box on my kitchen table," I said. "A friend is gathering the mail and putting it there for me to get, after I get home."

The bank helped me pay the bill over the phone, but now I had no credit card. I could use the debit card, but I kept the balance low. I could replenish the balance through the banking app on my phone, but it would be cumbersome, considering the lack of cell service in this area.

A further problem was that some of my utility bills had been auto-paid by the deactivated credit card. The companies would not have the new number in the payment options. It looked like a tangled mass of credit problems. At home a few phone calls would suffice. But out here on the trail, it promised to be a nightmare that I could not fix until I got home. All these financial matters were new to me. And I again became a bit miffed at Adnan for leaving me with such problems on my own.

One of my water bottles leaked too. I didn't realize it while in town. Too late. I would have to limp along until I could get a new one.

Back when Adnan and I were young, I knew that when I started to encounter obstacles in the way of my plans, I needed to change direction. Now I wondered if these problems were developing to tell me to go home.

Though my hiking energy seemed to be back in force, other little snags were unraveling my intention to hike the whole PCT too. Walking up a slope one afternoon, before I reached the town of Belden, I encountered smoke.

Where was it coming from? Had a forest fire flared ahead?

I found meager cell service and tried to call Tameem from the crest of a hill.

"I'm not where I can look online," he said.

I tried my friend Linda, who always seemed on top of any trail news.

"I'm driving," she said. "I haven't heard about any fire, but I can't look right now."

Fires had closed the trail in northern California before. *Would this be the obstacle that would finally send me home?*

Smoke on the horizon

CHAPTER 24

Done Walking

I SPENT A NIGHT BY myself on a ridge, wishing someone—anyone—would come along. As darkness fell, red and white lights blinked in the distance, clustered together, most likely a community in the foothills. I envisioned families sitting in a small café, talking, laughing, and eating together…and loneliness settled on my soul, like a deepening fog.

By morning the fog of depression had lifted somewhat, but I still felt the need of company. I packed to move north, perhaps to reach a town by night-fall. A brownish haze still obscured the far horizon, but I could not see a rising smoke plume.

Late that morning I noticed a pond below the trail, down a steep brushy slope. My water bottle was nearly empty, so I pushed my way between bushes on an animal path until I reached the edge of a bog surrounded by cattails. Sun glistened from the surface of the pond, and I could see a downed log where the water seemed deep enough to gather. I had to strain it through a bandana into the cook pot, as the water was murky with swirling mud, but my regular filter took the rest of the sludge out and soon I had clear water in my drinking bottle. I sat on the log, feeling refreshed. The smoke had not been able to reach this pristine place, and peace settled around my heart.

Knowing I had to keep going if I was to make any miles today, I climbed back up through the thickets of brush to where the PCT contoured the hills. Under a tall pine tree, in the middle of the trail, my eyes beheld something bright pink and yellow-green. *What was it?*

On closer inspection I found it to be a broken young pinecone with an intricate, sunray display of beauty. Most likely a squirrel had dropped it, but with so many available up high, it had not come down to retrieve it. How beautiful it was! I had never paid attention to the details of a pinecone's inner design before.

The loveliness of the morning lifted my mood and sent new thoughts to wriggle through my consciousness. Rather than dwell on the loneliness of widowhood, I should look to the next bend in my trail of life with wonder. Each curve of the path would have its own character to explore—whether on a dusty, gritty trail through mountains or on the invisible path through whatever lifetime was left to me.

Was this the final lesson I was to learn on my grief walk? Could I take this with me to add sparkle to my coming days without Adnan? I couldn't help thinking that the end of my trek was near.

As the baking heat of the day bore down on me, my energy dropped again. I arrived at paved Quincy-LaPorte Road, with an empty gravel parking lot on the far side. I crossed and slowly made my way up a side road to a PCT sign nailed to a tree, where the trail snaked upward in the oppressive afternoon heat.

I gratefully sat in the shade on the end of a weathered log without removing my pack, and I fished a plastic sandwich bag out of my cargo pants pocket. Inside it nestled a small pile of roasted almonds, which I ate as I gazed back toward the road. Two white vans ambled slowly by the parking lot and kept going down the hill toward Quincy. *Quincy! People existed there...and small cafés!*

I stood up with muscles that resisted movement in the sweltering air. My shoulders hurt. My feet hurt. My stomach was hungry, but it also felt ill from the heat and exertion. Still I forced my eyes and legs forward a few yards—just to the next downed log. There I sat again and looked back toward the road. A blue sedan cruised over the top of the hill and sped by on its way to Quincy.

Without my brain's permission, or intervention, my feet pushed me up and back to the parking lot where I crossed the road. I could not make myself hike north! Instead I started walking downhill at the side of the road. Cars and vans had passed this way. Surely one would stop to give me a ride to civilization.

Yes, there had been obstacles. But the morning had been beautiful, and that last epiphany that told me to discover new things and live with wonder seemed to tie a knot at the end of the grief walk. It seemed to tell me the end had come. I was done—done walking.

CHAPTER 25

Not Done Walking

ON THE WAY DOWN THE road to Quincy, I called Tameem, and he understood my decision. A few minutes later, though, I looked back up toward the top of the hill I had just descended on pavement. If I turned around, I could easily get back on the trail, and Tameem would be the only one who knew I had almost gotten off. But my body would not go back. It just kept walking down toward the town.

The phone rang. *What? Who would call?* The voice on the phone was that of my friend, Billy Goat, checking to see how I was doing. I thought I would be disappointing him by getting off the trail, but his words encouraged me to follow whatever my heart told me to do.

My feet burned from the hot, hard pavement. I was surprised to see so few cars, and it took five and a half hours before one stopped. A kindhearted man pulled his truck to the side and asked how far I was going.

"Quincy," I said.

"Hop in!" he said, and I was delivered to a motel in town.

After checking in I crossed the street to a local café, noting the families and groups of friends who sat together. Though I ate alone at a table by the window, I stopped to talk with one of the families, telling them of my loneliness on the ridge where I had seen the flickering red and white lights in the distance. I laughed with them as they included me in their lively conversation for a few minutes. How glad I felt to be among people!

My friend JoAnn drove two hundred miles to pick me up the next day, and another two hundred to bring me to her home for the night, full of generous hospitality. The following morning she took me to the airport in Medford, Oregon, so I could fly to Seattle and home.

Another bittersweet moment caught me by surprise as Tameem drove up to get me outside the baggage area of the airport in Seattle. The last time I had come in from a trip, Adnan had pulled up to the curb with his big, welcoming smile. This time Tameem was there with a warm greeting. I had to get used to these times. It seemed the first time I did anything without Adnan a little stab of sadness enveloped my heart, followed by the realization that he was gone forever. He would not be waiting at home or pulling weeds from the vegetable garden out back when I got there.

As it was I entered the silent house—still full of memories—and set down my pack. I slowly worked my way to the bedroom where Adnan had breathed his last breath. The hospital bed was gone, replaced by the old double bed we had used when we first got married, more than forty-eight years before.

His memories swarmed every corner of the empty house, but they flowed and changed with each aspect of the walls, ceilings, and floors. I remembered handing him tools as he applied paneling to the walls. As I looked out the window in the back bedroom, I could see the fig tree he had planted a few years before he passed away; it was laden with green figs. How he would have been pleased to see that!

Loneliness set in, especially at night, when I slept alone in our master bedroom. Never again would I have to wake him to stop his snoring. How I wished I could be lying there irritated by the noise again! How I felt guilty for having complained about it when he was alive.

With time I got used to the stabs of sadness when doing things without him for the first time. I went to a favorite restaurant with Tameem and his family, never before without Adnan. I got through it okay, and the next time I went, the sadness was not as strong. Still I could not go through his "oh my God" room (the one where he piled anything and everything he wanted to hide from guests) without the pain of permanent separation. One of his favorite shirts still hung on the door handle beside his file cabinet. His scouting memorabilia, still piled on a table next to the wall, sent swirling memories through me every time I glimpsed it as I walked by.

I filled my time with gardening to break the memory onslaught, but outside among the roses, more memories drifted around with the weeds. He and I had spent countless hours in the garden together, keeping it lovely. Now I could not even keep the weeds out. It was just too much work.

One day, Billy Goat called.

"How are you, Blue Butterfly?" he asked.

"I'm doing okay," I said.

"In October there's a hiker gathering in Massachusetts. Think you could come? Amoeba's having a 'pre-gathering' gathering at her farm, and she hopes you can make it."

I thought a moment. I had no commitments. I did not have to answer to anyone. I could stay out as late as I wanted without worrying anyone.

"Sure," I said.

He told me later he had not expected me to say yes, but that he was delighted with my answer.

And so I bought plane tickets and arranged for the trip. In Connecticut, where I landed and rented a car to drive to Amoeba's farm, another first gripped me with momentary sadness. I had never rented a vehicle on my own. Adnan and I had always been together for those occasions. It passed. And I entered a new phase of my life.

Most of the hikers at the gathering had hiked the Appalachian Trail (AT). I was a PCT hiker, but they treated me as if I was one of their own. I felt so warmly welcomed that I decided I wanted to hike the AT myself.

I was not done walking after all.

AFTERWORD

—◆—

THE NEXT YEAR I STEPPED out on the AT with hope for new experiences that would enhance my life, covering the old stories with new ones. The trail was different, but lovely. The people on the trail made a huge difference for me, keeping me from being lonely and making me feel alive. The trees, flowers, leaves, animals, and even the bugs brought new sights and sounds to enjoy.

Some things had not changed. I still had little jabs of sadness with the memories that poked up from the deep recesses of my brain from time to time. One such day I had come into a town for a rest day and sat at a table in an Italian restaurant. Soft music wafted out of the speakers in a corner of the room, and suddenly, a piece of music that had been popular during the time Adnan and I had first fallen in love with each other began its sweet melody.

Tears began to fall. That song cut through the framework of my recovery from grief and brought it to the surface. These moments of grief seemed to appear without warning. They would occur any place and any time, even after a couple of years had passed since Adnan's death. Others who had been bereft with losses told me they went through similar episodes. It seems I was following a predictable path through grief.

That year I stopped my hike at seven hundred miles to attend Asem's graduation from his surgical residency. I had strained my Achilles tendons on the steep hills of the AT, though, so I decided to give them a year to heal rather than to return to the trail and risk injury.

The following spring I started in Georgia once again to attempt the whole trail, all the way to Maine this time if I could. (By now I think I had become an adventure junkie!)

One day on the trail, I approached a rocky top of a hill and found a thru-hiker taking a rest. "Pony" was his name. I had a new pack made by a company in Germany with a yellow silk flower attached to a loop on the back.

"Is that flower real?" Pony asked.

"No, it's a Deuter pack," I said. "They put yellow flowers on all their women's packs, but it has special significance for me."

And I told him my story. I told him of the yellow flowers in Southern California, where the beautiful cluster of yellow wallflowers ruffled against my pant leg at the moment I thought I should not be out there, and it felt like Adnan was beside me, telling me that I was right where I needed to be. I told Pony that yellow flowers always reminded me of Adnan.

Continuing my story, I told him that when I reached Damascus, Virginia, the previous year, I needed a new pack. None of the packs on the floor of the backcountry store fit me. The clerk said there was a small women's pack in the back, and that it might work, so he went to get it. I watched as he brought it out, and a slight, internal shock registered through me as I saw a yellow flower dangling from the pack. *That* had *to be the* one. And it was.

"If I could give you a trail name, it would be 'Soulflower,'" Pony said.

Soulflower…I liked that name!

Rasheed, Asem, and Tameem stand with me in the kitchen a year and a half after Adnan's death. Kiara, who made Adnan smile during his last days, looks up from her daddy's side.

I will miss my sweet husband for as long as I live. I still go through periods of lonesomeness, especially when I see couples walking down a street, camping together, or riding on a plane side by side. I am alone, yet not really alone. His memories accompany me wherever I go, and my children and grandchildren do their best to fill my life with joy.

The lessons of the PCT eased me through some difficult times as a new widow. I am truly grateful for the chance to walk it, and for the good health that made it possible. Perhaps my experiences will help someone else who cannot walk the trail but can read my story.

As grief mellows, I keep putting one foot in front of the other on the path of life. May you, dear reader, find joy throughout your life and know that it exists, even in the dark times, somewhere, maybe just out of grasp, to eventually reenter and brighten your spirit.

Blue Butterfly/Soulflower

65685441R00084

Made in the USA
San Bernardino, CA
04 January 2018